A L H
2.5

This Was Radio

"Portrait of the Author as a Daring Young Man Performing from Memory—1944." (See Chapter 7.) Sketched at rehearsal by Staats Cottsworth on page of radio script.

Joseph Julian

This Was Radio

A Personal Memoir

Introduction by Harold Clurman

A Richard Seaver Book • The Viking Press • New York

Library of Congress Cataloging in Publication Data

Julian, Joseph.
  This was radio: a personal memoir.

  "A Richard Seaver book."
    1. Julian, Joseph.   2. Radio broadcasting—History.
PN1991.4.J84A37   791.44′028′0924 [B]   74-4805
ISBN 0-670-70299-4

Printed in U.S.A.

ACKNOWLEDGMENT

The New York Times: "A Plea For Better Radio Acting" by Joseph Julian.
Copyright 1944, Copyright © renewed 1972 by The New York Times
Company. Reprinted by permission.

To Lisl, who shared these years

In the Beginning Was the Wink . . .

Contents

Introduction by Harold Clurman

n *This Was Radio*, Joe Julian accomplishes a triple task. First, there is a great deal of information about one of the most influential of the media, one which we have all used, enjoyed, and learned from and about which most of us know very little. Second, Julian's book describes the atmosphere and moral landscape of the times during which radio came into being and flourished. *This Was Radio* is not only a personal but a social history. Third, all that the author tells us issues from a source that is not only truthful but pure. Radio and the people who contributed to its functioning come alive here: they are given a human face. And, what is more, the book is often very funny!

Because Julian writes from his own experience—without theory or doctrine—we find something symbolic and moving in his efforts to find a mode of expression. He is the universal actor struggling against all hazards and discouragement to find a place to practice his would-be profession. In doing this, we become sensible of a basic human need: man's desire at all times to manifest his inner self in a recognizably useful way. Julian strove with never-diminished determination to work at the job his nature clamored that he undertake. What makes this part of his story touching is that it is related not merely to the career of a single individual but to the contest all of us in one fashion or another must inevitably engage in. The cliché "hope springs eternal" is not just a sentimental wish, but a spur to action which is here made flesh.

When he "got going" and became successful as a radio actor, Julian took it seriously as a craft, and, even more, tried to extend it to the status of an art. In other words, he tried to enhance radio's effectiveness and relevance. In doing so, he not only became part of radio's most respected programs—in his association with Norman Corwin's famous play and documentary broadcasts—but as a result became involved in splendidly perilous adventures of world-wide reporting, which led him to England during the blitz and to devastated Japan immediately after the armistice. What he describes—without the boredom of statistical notation or routine observation—is not only vivid but memorably gripping. We cannot toss off the impression we receive from this account as so much "daily news." The simple directness of Julian's writing makes us feel we were there beside him, seeing what he saw and did and identifying with the sights he witnessed.

Julian was one of Joseph McCarthy's many victims, and throughout the book the episodes dealing with our local Cold War Inquisition of the 1950s are not only convincing on a personal level but heartbreaking, shamefully real on a national scale. How could we allow so much folly and injustice to occur among us? Reading these episodes, one feels that we failed to fulfill our responsibilities. Yet Julian, though bruised and sometimes appalled by all he has lived through, was not fatally scarred by these events. He never became bitter; his indignation is always softened by a feeling that virtue will in the last count somehow prove stronger than evil. This belief permeates and sets the tone of his whole book. Thus he is able in the midst of horror and viciousness to recognize and relish the comic. What he has seen and endured, however painful at times, has never debased his essential goodness. Another man with so close a view of our own men at war might have turned sour. Julian's instincts are healthy; his attitudes always remain uncontaminated by egotism or vindictiveness. For this reason we believe in him: all his true stories ring really true; he tells it "straight—like it was." The purity of his naïveté (to use his own phrase) is the mark of the book's good faith, verity, and value.

1. The Beginning

Nineteen thirty-two was not a thriving time for our cultural institutions. President Hoover was telling us prosperity was just around the corner, but that corner still seemed very far away. Large numbers of our population were drawing sustenance from breadlines; engineers and college professors were selling apples on street corners; and the theater was rapidly dwindling to a luxury for the rich, with thousands of actors out of work and hundreds clamoring for every role.

I was one of those thousands, fresh out of Baltimore, bent on carving out a theater career for myself, depression or no depression. A man named Cliff Self helped determine the route my theatrical career would take.

Cliff was an old-time Shakespearian actor, then in his late sixties. He had a thin, waxed mustache which he constantly twirled, and he walked tall. In his young years he had probably been a dashing leading man. Cliff built a nice little business out of a natural talent for gossip. He had developed a considerable reputation among actors for knowing what was going on in the theater. He used to hang around Broadway and Forty-fifth Street with other unemployed sons and daughters of Thespis, where he passed along casting tips and trafficked in general theater tittle-tattle.

When I arrived green in New York, certain only of future greatness, I hadn't the slightest idea where to begin; whom to see; how to go about making the rounds; or even where the rounds were. I knew, of course, that Times Square was the heart of the theater district, so I decided I would mosey about that area until I came across what looked like some actor types; I'd sidle up to them, eavesdrop on their conversation, and, hopefully, glean some idea about where to present myself to a casting director. That's how I met Cliff Self. He was hard to miss as an actor type.

With the Broadway and Forty-fifth Street set growing steadily larger, one day The Cliff Self Information Clearing Center asked himself the classic question: "Why not sell it instead of giving it away?" He rented a narrow, dingy room on the top floor of the Gaiety Theater building at the southwest corner of Broadway and Forty-sixth Street, stocked it with about twenty second-hand wooden chairs, an old desk, and an antique typewriter. Three large loose-leaf notebooks were his inventory. Every morning he would type into each notebook identical items of casting information—which producers were casting, what types they were looking for, where and when the interviews were being held, and other pertinent information. Many entries were culled from the theater section of the morning papers; others were gossip and tips from actors who had already investigated casting situations and returned to give Cliff a report.

Cliff charged twenty-five cents for a peek at one of the notebooks. That was his sole source of revenue, but word got around, and soon there were enough purchasers of peeks filing in and out to provide him a modest living. The place became a haven where unemployed actors rested from their weary rounds, read the trades—*Variety, Zits, Billboard*—and socialized and commiserated with one another. Huddling together was desperately needed to ease the pains of loneliness and self-doubt that acutely afflict idle performers. A painter can paint, a writer write, a composer compose when he wishes, and the muse is right. But actors, who, contrary to popular belief, have very fragile egos and are most vulnerable to rejection, are entirely dependent on others for the opportunity to practice their craft.

One of the prestigious radio programs of the day was *The March of Time*. It dramatized important news events of the week, and occasionally required extras for ad libs and crowd noises. At such auspicious times the producers would phone Cliff to send over six or seven unemployed actors, who would be paid five dollars each for their services. Cliff took no commission but dispensed this five-dollar bounty to his favorites. When the call came, he'd try to avoid hurting the feelings of the others present by signaling the chosen with an unobtrusive nod or wink, or a flick of his finger.

It was about two years after I started coming to Cliff's that I got my first wink. It was a great boost for my morale. The most exciting thing that had happened to me so far that year was being stranded at Sunbury, Pennsylvania, with a stock company that went broke after a few weeks and left the actors to get back to New York as best they could. Without enough for train fare, I obviously had a problem.

"Got any brilliant ideas, Smitty?" I asked George Livingstone Smith, our stage manager—a handsome, derring-do, Errol Flynn sort of fellow.

"We could always settle down in Sunbury," he said.

Sunbury is a town on the Susquehanna River, about fifty miles above Harrisburg. As we strolled along its banks, cursing our producer who had skipped town to avoid creditors, still wondering how we'd get back to New York on the five dollars and forty-five cents we had between us, Smitty had his illumination. Why not go back in a canoe? There was a number of old rowboats, flatboats, and canoes rotting away along the shore. Maybe we could buy one for a couple of bucks and fix it up. The trip would only take a few days and we'd have ourselves an adventure!

It sounded good to me. The Susquehanna emptied into the Chesapeake Bay at Baltimore, where my family lived. We could stop off there, then go on to New York. "The only thing is," I told Smitty, "I've never been in a canoe." He assured me that there was nothing to it, that he had many times shot the rapids in the rough rivers of northern Maine, and that the Susquehanna was a peaceful, lazy river like the Hudson or Mississippi.

We browsed among the wrecks until we found a canoe that must have belonged to Hiawatha. But since it didn't collapse under our test kicking, we went to the police station, told the desk sergeant of our plans, and asked him where we could find the owner. "Go on and steal it, boys," he said. "No one buys them things around here."

My clever friend cut up some canvas sandbags from backstage at the theater, to make patches. We bought some glue, and a can of paint, and lo, we had a vessel!

It was a miracle that we survived those next four days. My radio career almost never happened. The Susquehanna was *not* quiet and lazy. It's one of the most treacherous rivers in the country, full of hidden rocks, broken dams, and rapids. And as we hit our first white water, Smitty shouted above its roar, "Hey, Joe, I have a confession to make. This is the first time I've been in a canoe, too!"

We became experts the hard way: tipping over, losing a paddle, getting stuck on a bar of quicksand (I, idiotically, got out and tried to push us off, sinking to my nostrils before I was able to climb back in). Later, we were almost drawn over Holtwood Dam—a huge, electric power dam that spanned the river. My shipmate's ingenuity was responsible for that. Every four or five hours we had to beach the canoe to empty water that had seeped through the patches. At one place, Smitty was inspired by an old mattress lying on a dump. He pulled the cover off, cut some branches from a tree with his knife, lashed them together with a piece of rope, draped the mattress cover over this framework, and we had a sail. When I gathered the ends in my hands, stretched out my arms, holding the main pole between my knees, the wind caught us and zipped us gloriously over the bounding main. It was a thrill such as the person who invented the sailboat must have known—harnessing the elements to your purpose!

But it took us down river so fast that before we knew it we were only a few hundred yards from Holtwood Dam—a sheer 200-foot drop. We frantically killed the sail and paddled with all our might toward a little side reservoir, separated from the river by a stone wall. It had an iron ladder and railing running to the top. I lunged out and hooked it in the crook of my arm, just in time. If I had missed, we would have gone crashing over the dam.

Two men at a nearby powerhouse saw us and came running. They spun some wheels that opened a gate and pulled us into the reservoir, panting and exhausted. They took us and our canoe on a little electric train to the lower end of the river—state law requiring them to offer this service.

At night we slept in river town flophouses—for thirty-five cents a bedbug-ridden bed. We tried, with no luck, to catch our dinner by improvising a fishing line with a piece of rope and an open safety pin. We begged for food at farmhouse doors that were usually slammed—fearfully—in our faces. Where was all this famous country hospitality?

We really became disenchanted with our odyssey when the weather turned cold and violent. Cloudbursts filled the canoe with rain as fast as we could bail it out. We shivered and sneezed and were thoroughly miserable. That's when we decided enough was too much, and, in the full fury of an electrical storm, pulled ashore at Havre de Grace, Maryland, where we sold the canoe for three dollars to a local sucker and decided to hop a freight train the rest of the way home.

We found a "hobo jungle" just outside of town, where a couple of hospitable "'bos" invited us to dry out around their fire and share a tin of hot canned soup. I never experienced the brotherhood of man more intensely. The "'bos" told us that freight trains stopped there for a few minutes to take on water from a nearby tank. We socialized for a couple of hours until one arrived, then hopped into an empty car, with my one surviving, waterlogged suitcase. But as the train started up, we were shocked to see it going the wrong direction—north! Back up river from where we had so painfully come! As the engine picked up steam, Smitty jumped out and landed on his feet. I threw my suitcase out, then hesitated. The longer I hesitated, the more dangerous it became. I finally jumped—pragmatically, not bravely—and landed on my face in the cinders of the roadbed. I was a bloody mess.

Hours later we boarded a freight going south. As it got underway, we found we were sharing someone else's accommodation. A lot of people rode the freights in those depression years, sometimes entire families—the only transportation many could afford.

Our boxcar companion was a short, wiry character, who could have written a "How-To" book on the subject of freight-train-hopping. When he learned how I had damaged my face, he told me what I "shoulda done."

"Never take anything with ya ya can't strap on your back," he said. "So's you'll always have both hands free to hold on. And always have goggles to keep the cinders from the engine outa your eyes. An' if ya have to jump off, first start your legs movin' in the air, so's when ya land the momentum will keep ya runnin' on your feet. An' most important, before ya get in a car always look ta see if there's a woman there. If there is, run like hell! Don't go anywheres near her, otherwise the railroad dicks will grab ya under the Mann Act for transportin' a woman across state lines for immoral purposes. Even if ya never seen her before in your life."

About thirty miles from Baltimore, the freight train pulled into a siding and stopped.

We hitchhiked our last lap. Overall, it was the most frightening stretch of the trip. The man who picked us up was a genial, loquacious fellow. Though not quite sloshed, he was unsteady enough at the wheel to keep us gasping. The strain was unbearable until finally I fell back on pure faith. It got us home.

Back in New York friends smiled indulgently when I recounted my river adventure. I wouldn't have believed me myself.

I went back to making the rounds, and the daily visits to Cliff Self's tip factory.

That year, the closest I had come to a job on Broadway was selling shoes, part time, at Ansonia's on Forty-second Street. I earned barely enough to exist and frequently was hungry. When I was down to my last few pennies, I would go into a bakery and buy some leftover rolls. Several times a week I ate at Bernarr MacFadden's Health Food Restaurant. The famous physical culturist had opened a place off Times Square where you could buy a five-course meal for twelve cents. Each course was a whole-grain variation, which MacFadden insisted had all the required nutrients. My parents were dead, and although my adoptive family was fairly well off, I hated the idea of going back to Baltimore to live off them, face their "I told you so"s, and shoehorn myself into the family hat-store business for which I had neither appetite nor aptitude. But most of all,

I dreaded the prospect of abandoning my acting career before I had a fair chance to prove myself. So, when Cliff Self winked that day and I was convinced he wasn't winking at the actor next to me, I was more than elated. Radio drama was just beginning to come into its own. I had already knocked on a few doors but they wouldn't open. A relatively small group of actors seemed to be doing all the work: Everett Sloane, Dwight Weist, Vincent Price, Paul Stewart, Orson Welles, Kenny Delmar, Jeanette Nolan, Raymond Johnson, Ed Jerome, Agnes Moorhead, Clayton Collyer, Bill Adams, Richard Widmark, Carl Frank, Arlene Francis, among them. I learned later the reasons for the exclusivity, and why it was so difficult to break into this hallowed circle.

The March of Time used the same actors almost every week. It was like a stock company, whose members were the aristocrats of this relatively new profession of radio acting. They were extremely versatile, the nature of the show requiring of performers a wide variety of accents and characterizations and a talent for impersonation. Names in the news had to be counterfeited, and occasionally an outsider would be brought in. Franklin Roosevelt was president then. Bill Adams did a perfect imitation of him, which meant that he worked almost every show, since Roosevelt's name figured in the news almost every week. Art Carney, an excellent mimic, and Gilbert Mack also did the voice of FDR, and of many others. In fact, they were all so good many listeners believed they were listening to the real person.

Once, after playing Hirosi Saito, the Japanese ambassador to the United States, actor Guy Repp was summoned to the studio telephone. It was the Japanese consulate wanting to know why the Ambassador hadn't notified them he was in town. Repp explained he was only an actor impersonating Saito, but the caller was not to be put off. He insisted he was very familiar with the ambassador's voice and invited Repp to a diplomatic dinner the next evening.

Another time, Gilbert Mack's wife was at home listening to his voice coming over the radio as Franklin Roosevelt delivering his ringing Inaugural in which he said: "The only thing we have to fear is fear itself," when a man, who frequently stopped by to sell her fresh eggs, rang the doorbell. She hurriedly let him in, saying, "Shhh, I'm listening to my husband!" The man gave her a peculiar look and left—never to return.

Probably the strongest impression the listening population has retained of *The March of Time* is not that of the performers or of the content of the program but the frame—the stentorian billboarding of the opening and closing lines by announcer Westbrook Van Voorhis. I can still see him standing at the mike, legs apart, finger in ear (to hear himself better), launching those four words, "the march of time!" into space with the force of a howitzer. I'm sure they're still out there reverberating somewhere. That sound was too strong to have dissipated in a mere forty years.

My excitement was great as I reported that first day for rehearsals at the old CBS Studio A on the twenty-second floor of 485 Madison Avenue. Not only my first radio experience, but five bucks and working for one of the most important network programs! I knew I was just a crowd noise, but emotionally I was high. I had made it! My voice over a network, the length and breadth of the land! "Heard by millions!" I kept repeating to myself, "Heard by millions!" And when the director assigned specific lines to the extras so they would sound like a real crowd instead of a phony hubba-hubba babble, and gave me "Hey look, the guy's bleedin'!" my cup ranneth over. After rehearsal I phoned Baltimore and alerted the family to listen for that line. But, alas, no one was able to distinguish it from the rest of the crowd sounds even though, to stand out, I had hunched a few feet closer to the mike than I had been ordered to.

My performance on *The March of Time* did not catapult me to immediate fame and fortune. But Cliff Self liked me well enough to give me the wink every few weeks. Together with my part-time job at Ansonia's Shoe Store, I managed to keep my head above water.

It was frustrating to watch the regulars on *The March of Time* doing colorful, interesting roles while I was confined to a crowd noise. Envy gnawed at my heart, and a green voice kept whispering, "You could do it better, you could do it better!"

The next bit of good fortune that pushed my career along was the WPA—the Works Progress Administration—a federal program launched by Roosevelt's New Deal to create work for the unemployed masses, to provide a job for whoever needed one. Under the program, the famous Federal Theater Project was launched. Every actor who qualified as a professional was employed in some theater-connected capacity for twenty-three dollars a week. My Sunbury stock company experience qualified me (at least some good came from it). This was my first hint of what it meant to be independently wealthy. Twenty-three dollars was a lot of money in those days. I was assigned to travel around Manhattan organizing dramatic groups at churches and YMCAs. A few months later I was sent to WNYC, New York City's radio station, where I performed in sketches about keeping our streets clean, and occasionally spun records, filling in for veteran announcer, Tommy Cowan, who was probably radio's first disk jockey—at least for classical music. Tommy conducted the *Masterwork Hour,* and broke me in one day before he went to lunch. He handed me a pile of records and said, "Just announce them by reading the labels." I don't think any audience, before or since, has ever heard the names of the great foreign artists, composers, and conductors mangled so monstrously.

After a few months at WNYC I got my first Broadway acting job—a small role in Elmer Rice's *Judgment Day,* a highly effective courtroom drama based on the burning of the Reichstag by the Nazis. Rice was a distinguished, socially aware, American playwright. I knew him to be especially active on the side of the underdog. So I wrote him an underdoggy letter, bitterly complaining of the Broadway system. I reminded him how difficult it was for a young actor to get a job on Broadway, because Broadway producers only wanted actors with Broadway experience, and how can you get Broadway experience if no one will give you a job on Broadway without it?

He responded with a note inviting me to read for him. It was a hushed scene between two nervous guards conspiring against their government. I think my real nervousness played a big part in winning that audition.

We opened December 13, 1934, at the Belasco Theater, and for six months I earned twenty-five dollars a week, the Actors Equity minimum at that time. But the money, though desperately needed, was secondary. More important I had made it to Broadway! Forever after I shall have had Broadway experience! The thrill of being in a hit, of playing to Broadway audiences, the applause, the notable backstage visitors, was all very heady stuff. I remember being introduced to, among others, Gertrude Stein and Alice B. Toklas as they came back to visit one of the cast, Fania Marinoff. Fania, with her husband, Carl Van Vechten, was part of Miss Stein's Paris "family." Miss Stein was wearing a drab peasant-cloth coat that touched the floor. Much wider at the bottom than at the top, she left me with the impression of a gliding pyramid.

I had been granted a leave from the Federal Theater Project to do the play, so when it closed I went back to WNYC and skits about keeping the streets clean. But I did learn something of microphone technique there at New York City's own station, which helped me win an audition that was to be a big boost toward big-time radio.

In the mid-thirties WLW, Cincinnati, was the most powerful single radio station in the United States. Owned and operated by Powel Crosley, Jr., President of the Crosley Radio Corporation and owner of the Cincinnati Reds, WLW's 500,000 watts nearly blanketed the country. Apparently the government allowed that much power to one station as an experiment. In case of war or other emergency it could quickly take over and address the entire nation without arranging a complex hookup of smaller stations. Over the years WLW became known as "The Cradle of the Stars." Many of the biggest names in the entertainment world had their grounding there—Doris Day, Andy Williams, Red Barber, Durward Kirby, Rod Serling, Frank Lovejoy, Rosemary Clooney, among others.

Serving WLW's large audience required extensive programming and a large staff. One day in nineteen hundred and thirty-five Mr. Crosley just decided to clean house. He sent his general manager, Don Becker, to New York to interview and audition talent. Two weeks later he had signed up, for a year's work in Cincinnati, a full new complement of actors, announcers, writers, and directors. The reason for such a drastic shakeup, I suppose, was the station's rapid growth and the consequent need for more professional talent.

Becker had rented a large hotel suite and invited all who wished to apply for an audition and interview.

I chose for my audition my scene from Elmer Rice's *Judgment Day*, which I had played night after night for six months—material with which I was most secure. I think that's what gave me the edge.

My salary was to be fifty dollars a week, plus a few dollars extra for any sponsored program I worked on. I was on a four-week probationary period, after which the station could fire me if it didn't like my work.

In all, the new employees at WLW numbered about thirty. As we were being shown the facilities of the station, I struck up a conversation with one of the group, a writer-director called Thomas Ashwell. I was particularly impressed by his good looks, his quiet, assured manner, and easy charm. He told me he had recently worked at a radio station on the West Coast and that he intended to rise very rapidly here at WLW. He said he planned to do it by closely observing the way most employees related to the boss, Powel Crosley, Jr. If they were bootlickers and told him only what he wanted to hear, he would speak his mind. If they were forthright in their dealings with him, he would be a bootlicker. Either way, he said, by distinguishing himself from the others he would get ahead. It struck me as pretty cynical.

The numerous studios at WLW were of various sizes, to accommodate all kinds of productions. The larger ones were used mostly for musical shows with big orchestras and casts and heavy sound effect setups. The medium-sized studios were for smaller productions—dramas, recitals, interviews, and the like—and the smallest studios were mostly for news broadcasts and lectures. These last were the only studios without a piano and an organ. In those days, recorded music was rarely used. Orchestras and organists were "live." They set the mood and heightened emotional effects. Since music is the most direct of all the arts, it was of the greatest aid to an actor in quickly summoning a desired emotion.

And bars of music were the stagehands of radio, helping shift the scenery with a few suggestive notes. This music was often written and conducted by some of America's leading and most talented composers, such as Aaron Copland, Morton Gould, Bernard Hermann, and George Kleinsinger.

Among the dramatic shows on the air at WLW at the time of our arrival were: *The Life of Mary Sothern*, a typical daily soap opera; *Tea Leaves and Jade*, a lovely late-evening show that dramatized exquisite little fables and stories of the ancient Orient. Backed by low, exotic organ music, it used only actors with the most cultivated speech. *Famous Jury Trials* was a well-researched show that reenacted actual court trials. These had large casts, since both the prosecution and the defense usually offered a long string of witnesses.

Although on a weekly salary, the staff actors had no fixed hours of work. But we were always on call for any director who might want us for a show, or to audition for one. During my first few weeks I happened to get very few calls, either for auditions or direct casting.

Back to Thomas Ashwell. After *his* first few weeks, he concluded that most of the staff were bootlickers, so he walked into Crosley's office one day and told him that the majority of his programs stank. Crosley reacted by making Ashwell program manager.

Naturally a new program manager had to make a few changes. One of them was to fire some staff actors. I was among the chosen. Stunned, I stormed into Ashwell's office, angry and indignant. He was firm (an important quality for a man determined to get ahead). He said the record showed that I was one of the actors least in demand by the directors; hence I was not earning my salary. I told him I hadn't been there long enough for him to make such a judgment. He was charmingly pitiless.

I rushed in to see Don Becker, the station's general manager, for whom I had auditioned in New York. He was sympathetic, but felt that since Ashwell had just been appointed it would be wrong for him to countermand his order. I was furious. Where was justice? I had not even used up my four-week trial period. It wasn't that the directors didn't like my work, I told him, they just didn't know it. I hadn't been called to audition for the right roles. It was also a big financial slap in my face. I had spent the dregs of my bank account to attire myself presentably for my career at the station.

Becker began to relent. He said he'd see if something could be arranged. The next day he told me they were short an assistant sound-effects man, and asked if I would be interested in staying on in that capacity? Adding injury to injury, he told me the job paid only thirty-five dollars a week—a fifteen-dollar reduction. There was a short, sharp battle between my dignity and my need. I became a sound-effects man.

2. Siberia

Like music, sound effects played a major role in radio drama. They not only enhanced a play, but could set the scene. A few seconds of chirping crickets before the actors spoke bespoke a bucolic setting. Traffic noises immediately transported the listener to an urban locale. A mournful blast of a ship's horn, and he was down on the waterfront.

I had never actually worked sound effects before. I had observed a few things during my limited experience on *The March of Time:* the echo effect you can get by speaking across an empty water glass—the way Orson Welles did when, as "The Shadow," he spoke those immortal words, "Who knows what evil lurks in the hearts of men? The Shadow knows!" I knew that for horses' hooves you clomped half coconut shells on a tray of dirt or gravel; for gunshots you shot off blanks, or hit a leather cushion with a switch; for footsteps you walked on a board or slab of concrete. But there was, I soon realized, much more to it. Aside from having to learn all the tricks in the book—

manual and recorded—good sound men were also, of necessity, performers. Just as actors emotionally identified with their roles, so a sound man had to empathize and interpret. For a fist fight he was both men, busily smacking a fist into his palm, synchronizing the blows to the actors' grunts as they said, "Take that! And that! And that!" He had to feel along in a situation that culminated in a shooting, in order to time the shot perfectly. And he had to "die" with the victim in order to fall to the floor with the proper thud at the right moment. Footsteps, too, have their emotional context. Those of a woman walking off in a huff have a different sound and rhythm than they do if she is strolling or nervously pacing a hospital corridor awaiting the outcome of her lover's operation. A good sound-effects "performer" did not deliver these sounds mechanically. He often literally put on a woman's shoes and played the role. When it was a horse, he became the horse, slapping his chest for a gallop, changing rhythm for a canter, using the coconut shells for a slow trot, or pawing the ground— and throwing in an occasional whinny or snort for good measure.

I was usually the second man on sound effects, assisting with simple things when more than two hands were needed. But it was amazing the number of effects one good man could handle alone. Say the scene was about survivors on a life raft in the ocean during a storm. The sound-effects man would preset some recorded effects on the turntables, and, on a cue from the director, would twist a dial to bring up the sound of the roaring ocean, while the other hand would pull a lever on a crazy contraption that rubbed small pieces of dry leather together until they squeaked like the ropes binding the raft's logs. The first hand would now paddle in a water tank, giving a close-up sound picture of smaller waves lapping the raft. A quick twist of the control knob on another turntable and an airplane was flying overhead (would it see them and radio for help?). A vigorous shake of a large balloon full of birdshot produced a remarkably realistic effect of crashing thunder, which might be instantly followed by the sound of a man falling overboard—the splash made by the suction of a toilet plunger in the water tank.

The gyrations of a sound man coordinating such multiple effects at the peak of his efficiency and style was something to behold. It was, ladies and gentlemen, pure art.

It took me some time to develop a dexterity with even the easiest effects, like opening and closing doors. They were either too loud or too soft, maybe because, during my first weeks in "Siberia," I was still burning with resentment. It was intensely embarrassing for me to have to show my face as a sound man in the studio with my ex-fellow actors. Scar tissue hadn't yet formed over my humiliation. But I decided that if I wanted to hang on to even this job, I had damn well better stop being so churlish. So I drew on my acting talent to play the part of a sound man at peace with himself.

Actually, I became quite intrigued with the technology of sound effects, and with the imagination and infinite resourcefulness of the men who made them. At that time, increasing numbers of effects were being recorded for sound libraries, but the limitless variety of scripts constantly brought new challenges. And if there be a Valhalla where the souls of departed sound men gather to regale each other with their heroic earthly accomplishments, surely they will tell and retell of the time when a script of *Lights Out* (a late-night horror show originating in Chicago) called for the sound of a man being turned inside out. Due to insufficient demand, no such sound had ever been recorded. Thus it had to be created. After much experimentation, the masterpiece was achieved. It was a two-man job. One, very slowly, quarter-inch by quarter-inch, peeled a tight-fitting rubber glove from his hand, close to the microphone, while the other man slowly crunched a strawberry box for the sound of breaking bones.

The sound-effects department at WLW was headed by a true master of the art, Don Wingate. His virtuosity was clearly apparent in the way he handled emergencies. I remember the time, for instance, when, on his way to rehearsal carrying a stack of recordings of rifle shots, marching men, and the rat-a-tat-tat of machine-gun fire, the wheel of his motorcycle hit a rock and Don crashed. He wasn't injured, but the recordings were smashed beyond redemption. What to do? A lesser man would have committed suicide. These effects were vital to the show, which was slated to go on the air within a few hours. That was just about the time Wingate needed to round up an entire regiment of his buddies in the National Guard. They mobilized at the studio, replete with heavy boots and rifles, and after a brief rehearsal went on the air, marching about on cue, and since they had no blanks, shooting real bullets into the studio walls. They did little or no real damage because the padded, sound-absorbing walls were already porous. Now they were slightly more porous. Wingate hadn't been able to scrounge a machine gun from the National Guard, but that didn't daunt him. He got his rat-a-tat-tat effect by grabbing a short length of pipe and running it sharply across the studio radiator. For that evening alone, in my opinion, Don Wingate deserves an honored place in the Sound Men's Hall of Fame.

My first solo sound assignment was helping Red Barber, the sports announcer, perpetrate an innocuous fraud on the fans. One afternoon I was ordered to report to a small studio with a turntable and two effects—a recording of a crowd cheering and a bat smacking a baseball. When I arrived, Barber was sitting in front of a ticker-tape machine. It was ticking away, but no printouts were happening. It seemed to be marking time. Barber explained that the Cincinnati Reds' baseball game was about to start and he would be broadcasting a play-by-play description. Until I got the hang of it I should just watch him, and he would signal me when to bring in the effects.

I tested the crowd cheers and batted-ball effect, so that the control-room engineer could set his levels, then waited for the game to begin. The bat-clouting-a-ball effect was achieved without a ball. Only a bat and a leather-covered judge's gavel were used. No, I didn't strike the gavel with the bat. Holding the bat lightly by the neck, I smote it smartly with the gavel. The sound required was a violent contact of leather and wood, so it didn't matter which did what to which. This was the more practical way.

Waiting for the game to start, I tried to fathom why these effects would be needed in reporting a game over a news ticker in a tiny radio studio. Only when we went on the air did I understand that I was a co-conspirator in a plot to make listeners believe they were hearing a game brought to them directly from the stadium by an eyewitness reporter. As the ticker started spewing tape, Barber began transposing cryptic facts of plays that had already happened into colorful descriptions of these plays as they were happening. He did it with such conviction he almost had me believing I was at the ball park. He would embellish the factual information from the tape with vivid accounts of a player's behavior—gestures and actions that were sheer invention. For instance, the tape might read: THE COUNT WAS THREE AND TWO. THOMAS HIT A SINGLE TO CENTER. Barber would turn that into: "Three and two on Thomas now. He seems a little nervous, walks away from the plate, rubs his hands in the dirt . . . hefts his bat . . . coming back now . . . hunches over the plate . . . the pitcher wipes the sweat from his face with his sleeve . . . spits . . . winds up and here's the pitch!" Then he'd cue me to thwack my baseball bat with the gavel and turn up the crowd cheers. His enthusiasm and excitement would rise above the noise. "It's a good one! It's a good one!" he would shout. "A straight line drive to center field! There's the throw over to first . . . and the man is *safe!*" If it were a double or a triple, he'd yell even louder, signaling me for more decibels from the crowd. After a few innings I caught on, and naturally put the thwacks and cheers in the right places without being told. On a home run, I'd goose up the crowd as loud as I could and Red would give it full throttle, screaming his description of the ball soaring over the left-field fence many moments after it had already been there. A great sleight-of-mouth artist, Red Barber. But I trust Saint Peter won't hold him (and me) accountable at the gate of the Great Ball Park in the Sky.

After a few months in sound effects, I was surprised one day to be told to report for a dramatic audition. It seems they needed an Italian accent and none of the staff actors, at least none free at that time, could do it. I won the audition and played the role.

Several weeks later something similar happened. A director needed an eccentric voice, which he couldn't get from the available actors. Someone told him I did trick voices. He auditioned me and I did the show.

Shortly after that came a bigger surprise. I got a call from Thomas Ashwell, asking if I would have a drink with him that evening. I couldn't imagine what was up. Since he had fired me, our relationship had been quite formal, and, although I felt no real enmity toward him, we were never drawn to after-work socializing. My initial surprise became even greater when we met at a nearby bar; Ashwell told me he had a date later that evening, adding that his date had a girl friend. Would I care to come along? He assured me he would pay the tab.

I had a mixed reaction. Why me? Didn't he have any closer friends? I had an intuitive feeling I shouldn't go. I sensed something sinister. But, he was my boss; my livelihood depended on his good will; I also had a special curiosity about this man who had confided to me his curious plan for getting ahead. In a way I welcomed the opportunity to know him better. And, there was always the chance a blind date might turn out better than I dreaded. I agreed.

The girls were pretty but young—fifteen or sixteen— dangerously young. Ashwell had met them that afternoon on a streetcar, he said. They were working-class girls— spirited little sparrow types. We met them at the appointed place, a fairly sleazy no-cover night club on the wrong side of town, where they served good beer and bad strip-tease dancers. For several hours we watched and drank and made small talk. The girls giggled a lot, perhaps because their conversation was so limited, and I was sufficiently inhibited by their age to behave myself. Ashwell, too, was a model of rectitude. Apparently my intuition of evil had been all wrong. Not once did I see him even hold his girl's hand. He seemed perfectly content to enjoy the show and the girls' company. Along about midnight they said they had to get up early for work and thanked us for a good time. Ashwell hailed a cab, took their phone numbers, pressed a few dollars in their hands for fare, and we said good night. It was probably the most uneventful date I have ever had.

Ashwell suggested that we walk home. As we sauntered through a wooded park area back to "our" side of town, he opened up a bit. He thanked me for coming along. His wife and family were still out on the West Coast, and he said he was very lonely in Cincinnati. He even confided that his real name wasn't Ashwell. He used it, he said, to avoid being tracked down by some creditors he had left behind in San Francisco. Nothing serious, he added. He intended to repay them, but it would be an embarrassment if they located him here. I assured him I would tell no one.

As we were about to part company he suddenly said: "I want you back on the acting staff." Zing! The scab came off the wound. "Why?" I asked, in the tone of why-the-hell-did-you-fire-me-in-the-first-place?

He fumbled for an answer, said he was aware that I had been requested by directors, that my work had changed, and I would be more valuable as an actor. "How could my work have changed?" I demanded, "when I had previously done almost no work at all?" He didn't reply. I asked if my original fifty-dollar-a-week salary would be restored. He said no. "Okay, I quit!" came out without my thinking. "Okay, you get your salary back," he said just as quickly. He smiled. We shook hands and said good night.

The laws of compensation work in strange ways. The wrong of my demotion was redressed on the scales of justice. There had to be some connection between the way I was fired and the mysterious force that nudged the brain of the bookkeeper to correct, erroneously, my salary, not back to its original fifty dollars a week, but up to sixty-five dollars. I did not call the mistake to their attention. I figured that extra fifteen dollars compensated not only for my days of reduced salary, but for the mental anguish and humiliation I had suffered.

Without doubt, WLW was the best training ground in the country for radio actors. Its heavy programming made demands that were often challenges. Frequently miscast, I was nevertheless kept busy in a large variety of roles I never would have had the chance to play anywhere else. Occasionally they even had me read the news, which I invested with great feeling, emotionally involving myself with all the day's tragic events, until one day I was instructed to save my passion for my acting, and reminded that news reports are supposed to be dispassionate and objective.

After a year at the station I felt I had learned as much as I could there, and built up a big enough bag of experience to sling it over my shoulder and return to New York. Ashwell offered to renew my contract, but I felt my time was up. A number of directors I had worked for at WLW had already quit and were now directing shows in New York. I figured they would make good initial contacts.

(*Organ music in*)

And thus, at the age of twenty-six, young Joe Julian left WLW, grateful for all he had learned, and with his heart full of compassion for the listening population of Cincinati, which had to suffer what must have been the most exploitive of all station breaks anywhere in the world. Every fifteen minutes all day long, an announcer would say, "This is WLW, the Nation's Station, Crosley Radios and Shelvador Refrigerators, Cincinnati."

It was a tribute to the tolerance of listeners that the station was never firebombed.

3. Return to New York

New York did not exactly welcome me with open arms. My contacts from Cincinnati were delighted to see me and would keep me in mind. The competition from other actors trying to break into the big time was terrific, but I assiduously made the rounds every day, which meant hounding the casting departments of the networks, advertising agencies, and production houses that produced radio programs.

Auditions were frequently held for new roles, but the casting departments mainly called the "charmed-circle" actors to compete with one another. There were leftover parts, however, and as more and more dramatic shows went on the air, unknowns and near-unknowns did get their chance. We somehow had to wangle an audition or an interview with the casting people. This was done mostly by sheer, obnoxious persistence—bombarding them with letters, visits, and phone calls. Others used the ambush technique, grabbing directors (sometimes literally) as they came out of the studios when their shows

went off the air. The third-floor lounge at NBC in Rocke-
feller Center was a favorite ambush point. One actor might
suddenly step from behind a pillar. "Oh, hello, Mr. Vincent," he'd say, feigning surprise at seeing the director,
but thus hoping to register in his consciousness. Others
were more blunt. "Anything for me in your next show, Mr.
Brown?" "It's been a long time since I worked for you,
Mr. Andrews." "You told me to keep in touch with you,
Mr. Ricca." Smart directors sneaked out the back way.

I, too, lost no opportunity, exploited every contact that
might lead to a job or an audition. And, as the money I had
saved ran low, I became as obnoxiously persistent as the
best (or worst) of them.

Finally, after about six months, one director who had
known me at WLW, and whom I had badgered unmer-
cifully, called me for a running part on *The Life of Mary
Sothern,* a serial that had just moved from Cincinnati to
New York, and simultaneously I was called for a one-time
part on the popular *Myrt and Marge* serial for the very day
I was to begin. The air times of these shows were fifteen
minutes apart—but rehearsal calls overlapped. It never occurred to me to turn down the second job. I had struggled
too hard for a breakthrough. The gods were rewarding me
for my perseverence; they would be displeased if I refused
any part of their sudden bounty. I decided to do what busy
actors frequently did when they had a time conflict.
They'd hire an actor to stand in for them at a rehearsal,
while they ran to another studio for a performance of a
show that had been previously rehearsed, then back again
to do the first show. If the directors were amenable, it
worked out fine for everyone, including the stand-ins, who
not only got five or ten dollars but an opportunity to dem-

onstrate their talent to directors who might not know their work.

My stand-in arrangement was approved. But then I suddenly realized how far apart the studios were. *Myrt and Marge* was on the twenty-first floor of the CBS building, at Madison Avenue and Fifty-second Street, and went on the air at 2 P.M. *The Life of Mary Sothern* was on the seventh floor at Broadway and Forty-sixth Street and went on the air at 2:15. I was only in the first part of the first show and the middle section of the second—about nine and a half minutes to get from one place to the other. Could I make it? I tried it out. Even by running part of the way, I arrived exhausted, over three minutes late, and in no condition to do a broadcast.

What to do? I had already accepted both jobs. An ambulance! I plucked a number from the Yellow Pages and asked how much. The man said twelve dollars. When he learned I was not an invalid he said it would be fifteen. Why the difference? "For the risk," he said. "It's against the law to carry a non-invalid."

I arranged to have him waiting at CBS. I tipped the elevator operators in both buildings to have cars waiting for me. I finished my part on *Myrt and Marge,* slipped out of the studio and rushed to the waiting elevator—which wasn't waiting. The operator had forgotten. I almost broke my thumb pressing the "down" button. When the elevator finally came, over two precious minutes had been lost.

The ambulance was out front. To casual onlookers, it must have seemed strange to see a man racing to an ambulance rather than being carried to it. I told the driver to get going.

"Lay down," he said. "Ya gotta lay down." I stretched

out on the white slab. "Listen," he said, "crosstown traffic is pretty bad. I could get stuck even with my siren. I
think we're better off going up Madison, across Fifty-
seventh and down Seventh Avenue. It's longer, but the
streets are wider and we'll make better time. How about
it?"

"Okay, okay, just get moving!" I said.

He started off, the siren winding up to a howl, then a
scream. I couldn't resist half-sitting up to watch the cars in
front of us jam on their brakes or pull to one side. For a
brief moment I forgot my urgency as I absorbed some of
the siren's power. It was all for me! It activated some resi-
due of childhood megalomania.

"Lay down!" the driver yelled. "Ya wanna get me arrested?"

My panic returned. Every few seconds I'd pick up my
head to check our progress. "Faster, faster!" I kept urging.
"Stay down!" he kept answering. We swung around into
Fifty-seventh Street at 2:13. The traffic was lighter there
and at 2:14 we turned down Seventh Avenue. At which
point the siren broke.

"Look," the driver said, "I can stop and fix it, but it will
take a few minutes. Or I can take a chance on going
through without it. What should I do?"

"Take a chance!" I shouted. We still had four minutes to
make it. The traffic was heavier now, but he pushed ahead,
going through red lights. There was a near miss at every
crossing.

We finally pulled up in front of Loew's State Theater
building, at Broadway and Forty-sixth Street—where the
WHN Studios were located—with only two minutes to
spare. Again, it must have perplexed the crowd to see a

man leap from an ambulance bed and run like a bat out of hell into the lobby, where this time the elevator *was* waiting. It took me express to the seventh floor. I ran down the hall and dashed through the studio door. In unison, the director and the entire cast let out a huge, silent groan of relief. They were on the air. Someone shoved a script into my hand. I took one gulp of breath—and spoke.

I received twenty-three dollars for the *Myrt and Marge* job. The ambulance was fifteen. Five for the stand-in. Add a buck a piece for the elevator operators. One dollar profit. Add the wear and tear, and it came out a loss. But it really was a net gain; it taught me never to try anything like that again.

Gradually I began getting more auditions—and winning a few now and then. I picked up isolated jobs on shows like *Flash Gordon; Inner Sanctum; Joyce Jordan, Girl Interne;* and *Renfrew of the Mounted.*

Waiting in the studio for a *Renfrew* rehearsal to start, I got into a conversation with a tall, distinguished-looking gentleman named Brad Barker. In the middle of an animated discussion of the philosophical implications of Kant and Hegel, he suddenly excused himself, walked over to a large cardboard cylinder mounted on a metal frame, put his mouth to one end, and emitted the blood-curdling howl of a timber wolf, which was the opening signature of *Renfrew of the Mounted,* a weekly series of half-hour stories of Canada's legendary Royal Canadian Mounted Police—sagas of manhunts and battles between the good guys and bad guys in the Canadian wilderness.

Barker (what's in a name?) was one of a small group of specialists who made a good living doing animal sounds, baby noises, and screams—which were always in demand.

The animal imitators could come up with just about anything asked of them, from the chirp of a pregnant canary (any age) to the roar of a distempered rhinoceros.

Donald Bain, one of the best, would be meowing and barking and spitting, as both characters of a cat and dog fight. You risked getting drenched if you stood too close. Some actors once played a dirty trick on him. They accompanied him to the Automat, where he regularly had lunch, then one telephoned from the outside and had him paged. Pretending to be the director of a radio show, he told Bain that he needed someone in a hurry who could do a good cat and dog fight, and that he had been recommended. Would he be willing to do a short audition over the phone? Whereupon Bain furiously snarled and meowed and spat and barked into the receiver, while everyone in the restaurant roared at the antics of this seemingly demented little man.

The baby criers were usually women, who carried a small pillow around with them, into which they gurgled, whined and bawled. Sometimes they would also lisp the words of a young child.

The screamers? You might think anyone can scream? Not so. 'Tis an art. There are all kinds of screams: some that are short and eerie, others that are long and shrill. And screams you might hear in a Gothic tale, of the victim before the kill. Some screamers were better than others, but they all saved the throats of the actors for whom they doubled, enabling them to continue the performance without hoarseness.

The most powerful casting director at that time was Frances von Bernhardi, who worked for Frank and Anne

Hummert, an incredibly successful husband-and-wife team that dominated the field of radio drama. Former journalists, they pioneered the format of the daily series and suffused them with the same low common denominator—sentimentality—that characterized the publications of their former employer, William Randolph Hearst. And, like Hearst, they grimly dominated their empire. When they'd suddenly appear to watch a dress rehearsal of a show, the atmosphere in the studio immediately chilled. All chattering ceased. Actors would twist their faces into rubbery grimaces while silently moving their lips, to demonstrate how diligently they were studying their roles. There was something darkly foreboding about the Hummerts. Their stiff presence always evoked a sense of insecurity. And with good reason. They had a reputation for firing actors who incurred their slightest displeasure. And authors. When Mrs. Hummert once told a writer that she wanted "God" on every page of a script, and his answer was "Who will we get to play Him?" he was fired on the spot. And when you were fired from one of their shows it was a catastrophe. It meant being banned from *all* their nine or ten others that might be on the air at any given time.

I once barely skirted such a fate. It was a wintry morning, I had overslept and arrived for a nine o'clock dress rehearsal not a few—but twenty—minutes late. This was a day of double jeopardy, because, in addition to the Hummerts being present, Martha Atwell was the show's director. Miss Atwell was a tight-lipped spinster who was an absolute fanatic on punctuality.

As I entered the studio the entire cast and orchestra were in position, waiting. They glanced at me, then averted their eyes, not wanting to witness the bloodletting.

The atmosphere was thick with tension. I looked up at the control room, where the engineer and three stony faces scowled down at me as they awaited my explanation. I gulped, took a folded piece of paper from my pocket, and without a word went into the control room and handed it to Miss Atwell. Then I returned to the studio, where I looked up to watch her face. When she had finished reading the note, she shot me a look, then handed it to the Hummerts, who glanced at it—and burst out laughing. Miss Atwell joined in and the danger was over. The note I had scribbled on my way to the studio read:

Dear Miss Atwell,

Please excuse Mister Julian for being late. On accounta the snow storm I had a hard time gettin' him a cab.

Yours very truly,
The Doorman at his Building.

I was not only glad to have escaped their wrath, but to learn that a sense of humor was still alive behind their dour exteriors.

These are a few of the five-days-a-week serial dramas Frank and Anne Hummert produced:

Amanda of Honeymoon Hill
Backstage Wife
David Harum
Evelyn Winters
Front Page Farrell
John's Other Wife
Just Plain Bill
Lora Lawton
Lorenzo Jones
Mrs. Wiggs of the Cabbage Patch

Nona from Nowhere
Orphans of Divorce
Our Gal Sunday
Real Stories from Real Life
The Romance of Helen Trent
Second Husband
Skippy
Stella Dallas
The Stolen Husband
Young Widder Brown

In addition to these daytime "soaps," they had a number of prime-time evening shows such as *Manhattan Merry-Go-Round; Mr. Chameleon; Mr. Keen, Tracer of Lost Persons; Hearthstone of the Death Squad.*

The Hummerts themselves usually dreamed up a show's original concept, building it around a folksy or easily identifiable character. They employed a large stable of writers. One group worked exclusively at developing story lines and plots. When approved by the Hummerts, the scripts were passed along to the dialogue writers. There were many do's and don't's. For instance, all characters had to be constantly identified by name:

JOHN: Why, hello, Henry!
HENRY: Hello, John.
JOHN: Haven't seen you in a long time, Henry.
HENRY: Yes, that's true, John.
JOHN: How about joining me for a drink, Henry?
HENRY: Why, I'd like to, John.

Unnatural? Yes, but they felt it was essential to know who was talking to whom at all times. They must have thought their listeners were pretty stupid not to be able to tell from the dialogue itself.

Plot lines were often altered by a performer's real-life situation. Some contracts provided they be written out of the show for a few weeks in order to rehearse a Broadway play. The writers would then invent a reason for the character's disappearance. Perhaps he would be sent on a journey abroad, or to a rest home, or, perhaps, to jail. The same when an actor took sick. And, if he suddenly quit or was fired, there were always easy ways of killing him off—a heart attack, an auto accident, a murder. But this was generally done only with supporting characters who were expendable. If one of the leads left the show, he was usually replaced by another performer. Over the years, in long-running serials like *The Goldbergs; Jack Armstrong, the All-American Boy;* etc., many actors played the same part.

Long pauses could never be indicated in a script. "Dead air" was anathema, the theory being that during even a five-second silence, a hundred thousand listeners might be just tuning in. Hearing nothing, they'd turn to another station, losing all those customers for the sponsor's product.

To snag new listeners, and for those who may have missed a chapter, each episode of a serial had to be preceded by a short recapitulation of the plot:

ANNOUNCER: Yesterday, we left Alice in her living room, alone with John Hennesy, her sister Gwendolyn's husband. John had just confided that he had always been in love with Alice, and had made a terrible mistake in marrying Gwendolyn. Gwendolyn, who had left the house moments before, suddenly remembered she had forgotten some books she wanted to return to the library. As she reentered the living room, John had just put his arm around Alice's waist. Gwendolyn froze as she heard John say:
JOHN: Darling, I love you more than anything in this world!

This would be followed by a music sting (*Sharp chord*), the organ music would fade, and the announcer would come in with the first commercial. Generally there was an opening, middle, and closing commercial—a terrible price that listeners didn't seem to mind paying for their addiction to "soaps."

Frank and Anne Hummert closely supervised every show, at all stages. Their entire operation was highly systematized, and scripts were turned out with the efficiency of an assembly line.

The Hummerts' casting director, Frances von Bernhardi, a rather severe career lady, seemed cut from the same cloth as her employers. Perhaps that's a little unfair. I did sense an underlying warmth. She may have acquired some of the characteristics of this Victorian couple after years of close association. In any case, with all those parts to fill in all those shows, she wielded a lot of power. Actors were careful not to offend her. She was totally devoted to her work and differed from most casting directors in that she not only arranged auditions but kept close tab on the general deportment of performers. Too much clowning or lateness to rehearsal could lead to reprimands. An item in the paper linking an actor to some scandal might well result in the actor being replaced. All talent and other employees, as well as the material on their shows, had to adhere to the Hummerts' rigid moral code, and woe unto the transgressors. But despite all the above, the Hummerts were loyal to their actors. Whenever possible they kept the same ones working on all their shows.

I managed to get a toe in the door of the Hummert empire by winning small roles in a couple of their programs: *Chaplain Jim*, which dealt with the spiritual problems of

GIs in Army camps, and *Front Page Farrell,* the dashing exploits of a super reporter (played by Richard Widmark).

By the late thirties network programming had pretty well standardized its form. Its main categories—drama, comedy, and music—were served up in quarter-, half-, and one-hour slices of time.

Most of the dramas were, of course, the daytime "soaps"—so called because they were listened to mostly by women while doing their washing and cleaning, who were thus presumably vulnerable to sales pitches by the soap company sponsors. The essential ingredients of these shows were nicely contained in James Thurber's definition of a soap opera:

> A kind of sandwich, whose recipe is simple enough, although it took years to compound. Between thick slices of advertising spread twelve minutes of dialogue, add predicament, villainy, and female suffering in equal measure, throw in a dash of nobility, sprinkle with tears, season with organ music, cover with a rich announcer sauce, and serve five times a week.

In the evenings dramas were always on the menu, but the emphasis was on comedy and music.

Most of the important comedians sprang full-blown from vaudeville—especially those whose speciality was essentially non-visual, such as the joke tellers: Lou Holtz, with his ethnic stories of "Sam Lapidus"; George Jessel and his "Hello, Mamma?" phone routine; Jack Pearl's Baron Munchhausen. They and other vaudevillians such as Eddie Cantor, Jack Benny, Bob Hope, Bob Burns, Burns and Allen, Jimmy Durante, Abbott and Costello, and Ed Wynn, often carried their visual gimmicks with them into the radio studio via publicity photographs. The jokes were funnier if listeners retained the image of, say, Joe Penner's baggy pants, or of Eddie Cantor rolling his "banjo eyes", or of Ed Wynn's mugging and goofy hats.

The weekly audiences for these comedians jumped abruptly from a few thousand in vaudeville to multi-millions in radio. Their catch phrases, such as Jack Pearl's "Vas you dere, Sharlie?" Penner's "Wanna buy a duck?" and Jimmy Durante's "Goodnight, Mrs. Calabash, wherever you are" were heard so often they became part of the culture.

But these comics paid a price for their new popularity. In vaudeville, a comedy routine lasted for years; in radio, it was consumed in a night. The strain of building a new show every week took its toll, and there were many breakdowns and retirements and comebacks among the nation's top funny men.

Laughter is lifeblood to a comedian, and many found it difficult telling jokes to a microphone that wouldn't laugh. The first stage show ever broadcast featured Ed Wynn in *The Perfect Fool,* over station WJZ, February 19, 1922. He was appalled at the silence after he told his first, time-tested jokes. He asked the announcer to quickly round up anyone he could find around the studio. A short while later he regained his confidence as an audience of maintenance men, telephone operators, electricians, and cleaning women giggled and howled at his silly sallies and facial expressions. Studio audiences became a must for comedy shows.

There was also a kind of humor indigenous to radio. Mock insults and feuds between two leading comedians would boost each other's ratings, and sometimes could be kept running for months, such as the one between Jack

Benny and Fred Allen, in which Allen kept finding new ways to describe Benny's stinginess. One evening a sketch had Benny being held up by a thief who snarled, "Money or your life!" The long, long period of dead air that followed became hilarious, and was topped by Benny finally saying petulantly, "I'm thinking it over." This just couldn't be as funny in any other medium. And there was Allen's classic retort to an insult by Benny: "If I had my writers here you wouldn't talk to me like that and get away with it!"

Speaking of comedy, probably the most unique comedy performance in radio history occurred in 1937 when, during a newspaper strike, the mayor of New York City, Fiorello H. La Guardia, took to the air to read funny papers to the children. The kids "didn' wanna know from nothin' " about wages and working conditions—they missed their funnies! La Guardia, mayor of *all* the people, understood what that deprivation meant, and every evening, for as long as the strike lasted, he would act out all the parts in his high squeaky voice and slight lisp, gesticulating dramatically as he described the pictures and read the ballooned dialogue of the comic strips that regularly appeared in the New York papers. It was something to hear—and behold. Fiorello La Guardia, or "The Little Flower" as he was affectionately known, was a mayor who cared.

But music was also very much in—or on—the air during the thirties, catering to all appetites.

The National Barn Dance was a Saturday night fling for millions of farm folk and lovers of country music. Some of the popular big band leaders were Paul Whiteman, Fred

Waring and his Pennsylvanians, and Ben Bernie (The Old Maestro—"Yowsah, yowsah, yowsah . . ."), and some of the top variety shows were *Your Hit Parade, Show Boat,* and *Kraft Music Hall.*

Outstanding female vocalists of the period were Dinah Shore, Jessica Dragonette, Ruth Etting and outsized Kate Smith (whose singing signature, "When the Moon Comes Over the Mountain," brought one of radio's sunniest personalities into our living rooms.

Among the popular male singers there was a handful of strong, lyric voices like those of James Melton, Morton Downey, and Arthur Tracy ("The Street Singer"). And then there were the crooners—Bing Crosby and Whispering Jack Smith, who probably started it all. Or was Rudy Vallee to blame?

Crooning can probably be best described as the opposite of Ethel Merman. It was a style of singing romantic ballads that tried for maximum effect with least expenditure of energy; the microphone became a prosthetic device giving artificial power to those without enough of their own. The invention of the microphone bred a large race of mike-dependent singers whose natural voices would never have reached the balcony of a vaudeville house in those days when a singer needed not only a pleasing tone but a healthy pair of lungs.

Even today in television, while the voices of singers are electronically boosted, the microphone itself is a barrier between the artist and his audience. We have the technology to send a man to the moon, but apparently science has not yet found a way to engineer a song without the silly spectacle of the singer half hiding his face as he holds a metal cone to his mouth and throws a slack wire around, stepping over it like a cowboy doing a rope act, while he deludes himself and his listeners that the big sound he is making is all his own.

Those with deeper hungers were rewarded occasionally with arias from the thrilling voices of Lawrence Tibbett, Lily Pons, Rosa Ponselle, and other opera stars. On Saturday afternoons entire operas were broadcast live from the Metropolitan Opera House. And there were regular live concerts by the NBC Symphony—one of the finest in the land—from Studio 8-H in the RCA building.

Whenever I was rehearsing a show on the same floor, I would run out at every opportunity and sneak into 8-H to watch Arturo Toscanini rehearsing his concert. It was a show in itself. His men worshipped him, but the Maestro was very temperamental. He demanded perfection of his musicians, and when he didn't get it he exploded. One day he had such a violent reaction to a note wrongly played that he threw a valuable gold watch onto the floor and smashed it. The next day, during a break, a messenger delivered a package to him from David Sarnoff, the president of RCA. He opened it and found two one-dollar Ingersoll watches—with a card reading: "For rehearsals only."

4. The "Variety" Storm

Although I began winning more radio auditions, my heart was still in the theater. I continued to make the rounds of Broadway producers, took classes in improvisation and body movement, and wormed myself close enough to the famous Group Theater to land a small role in one of its last and most beautiful productions, William Saroyan's *My Heart's in the Highlands*. It ran for six months and rekindled my yearning to make the theater my way of life. Continuity of stage work was rare for any actor, but I redoubled my efforts and did come up with a part in another Broadway play, *Walk Into My Parlor*. It ran three weeks.

Most theater people sneered at radio actors. The very term became one of opprobrium. It was too easy just walking up to a mike and reading from a piece of paper. I myself was prone to the same prejudice, thinking of it as fractional acting, a nice way to make a living while waiting for the big break in the theater.

For the very busy actor it was more than a living. Money was to be made. Without sweat. Real money. The last

Klondike of the profession, B.C. (Before Commercials).
Actors who had running parts in several daily "soaps"
might make up to $1500 a week—more than many well-
known stage and screen personalities made. These could
work in only one production at a time, but a versatile radio
performer could and often did play a half dozen parts in a
single day. A lead on a daytime serial could be contracted
for from $1200 to $2500 a week. In addition, many worked
the nighttime dramas. So some radio actors were making
$50,000, $75,000, even six-figure salaries in an era when
the average yearly wage was around $3,000, and taxes
were much lower than they are today.

As I became more and more one of the "in" group, I
began to understand why it was an "in" group: radio acting was not as easy as it looked. Many excellent actors
were incapable of developing the necessary technique. It
was largely a technique of indicating emotions, or playing
"results"—anathema to serious actors who cannot perform
until they have assimilated the truths and depths of a role.
There is no time for that in radio. A typical half-hour program had to be put on with only three or four hours of rehearsal. Performers had to produce quickly. The good ones
developed a facility—a bag of tricks which enabled them
to give effective performances. But it was all partial: partial emotion, partial characterization, partial truth. They
leaned heavily on the listeners to complete their acting for
them. And the bag of tricks was acquired at a cost. In my
opinion, the busier actors became in radio, the more they
degenerated as creative artists. It was typical that so many
radio actors, after winning auditions for roles in stage plays
by impressing with facile first readings, had to be fired
during rehearsals because they were incapable of going

any further, adding new dimensions to their roles. In fact, they usually got worse under the pressure of having to deliver with their entire being.

I observed this creative decay not only in others but in myself, and it disturbed me. I pondered the question for some time, then shaped my thoughts into an article and mailed it to *Variety*, the weekly bible of show business. To my surprise it appeared in full the following week, January 15, 1941.

AN ACTOR ANALYZES RADIO ACTING
Sees Broadcast Drama As A Director's Medium
By Joseph Julian

Radio dramas, which are poured out into the ether in unending profusion, have soaked up a large part of the unemployment slack among the Actors Equity Association members. They've created work which has enabled many actors to carry on in the face of a more or less permanent Broadway job famine, and provided many of them (especially bit and supporting players) with steady incomes and a security the theater has never offered. But aside from the financial and psychological values of a more constant employment, what has been the effect of radio on the actor as a creative artist?

Much has been written and said of the growth of radio, of its development as an art form, of the ever-increasing number of adult programs. It has made great strides. It is persistently enticing the best talents from the other entertainment fields—actors, directors, and authors. But while to directors and authors it is a fascinating new medium to explore, experiment with, and study, to actors it presents a direct challenge to their artistic integrity.

NOT ACTOR'S MEDIUM

If a survey could be made of all actors working in radio who came from the theater or film lots, and if some kind of test were possible to gauge their "then and now" abilities, it would un-doubtedly show most of them to have been better actors then than now.

There are many reasons for this, but they all boil down to the fact that radio is essentially a director's, not an actor's, medium. An actor grows and develops best working where he is afforded the best opportunity for a full performance—in other words, on the stage, with motion pictures second and radio dragging up the rear.

The stage, with its physical production limitations, necessarily relies most on performers. Films call for little hunks of act-ing at a time, with the cutting room polishing off the perfor-mance. And the motion picture camera with its broader scope largely usurps the function of the actor by subjective treatment of a story. For instance, it can give a value and significance to m'lady's dropped handkerchief by isolating it (the hanky) with a closeup. Or, when the furious waters of the river drag our hero's canoe closer and closer to the onrushing falls, it adds suspense by cutting in with a shot of the jagged rocks below. All of which amounts to the director talking to the audience in-stead of the actor.

THE BRUTAL MIKE

The radio microphone, from the creative actor's point of view, is even more brutal. It must achieve its effect entirely with sound. Sound is only one dimension of a performance, and an actor in a radio drama cannot possibly translate into sound all the active, silent nuances, bits of business, gesture, pauses, without becoming aware of what he is doing, thereby working consciously for an "effect" or a "result," which always spells bad acting.

Most of the better actors are conscious, I think, of a lack of inner satisfaction after doing a radio job. They miss that sense of fulfillment so vital and nourishing to any artist, and it usually shakes their confidence in themselves, undermining the talent they have. Others hold the general low level of writing, pro-duction and insufficient rehearsal time responsible. While these are contributing factors, there are causes more basic. It's true that an actor can do more with a well-written script than a badly-written one. And it's true that in spite of the remarkable progress radio writing has made; in spite of the "Corwins" and the "Arch Obolers," corn still runs rampant on the airwaves. But we can look forward to better and better scripts. We can look forward to adequately rehearsed programs. Actors may even memorize their lines instead of reading them. Freed from the necessity of keeping eyes glued to a script, they'll better adjust to their fellow actors. Perhaps they will work their own sound effects to give them a better feel of situation and circumstance (opening and closing their own doors when supposedly entering a room, etc.). We can even look forward to technical improvements—mobile microphones that will follow the actor (as in film making), allowing him freedom to move and behave more naturally than the present stationary mikes, which confine his movements to a narrow "live" beam, and inhibit all his naturally felt gestures. In a love scene, for example, if he could cross to his fair one, take her hand gently in his own, look longingly and deeply into her eyes before saying "Darling I'd go to hell and back for you," it would certainly come over the air with a greater ring of truth than if he would say, as he now must, to a cold, unresponsive microphone, with script in hand, one eye running down the page to find the next line, the other glancing at the director for cues and to see if he should speak faster or slower (so the program shouldn't run a second under or over time), and generating all of his inspiration from his own mental images of the girl and the situation. Even these images are at best blurred ones. Because the high degree of concentration necessary for an actor to keep a clear, strong image in his mind is not possible under such conditions.

ARTISTIC STAGNATION

However, even though all these improvements come about, radio acting would still induce artistic stagnation and disintegration in the creative performer because of limitations inherent in the medium itself. Take the "fade-out" and the "fade-in," for example. These are the stagehands of radio. They're the devices that shift the scenes. In the theater, during scene changes, the actor has several minutes at least to inwardly prepare himself for the next scene. In making a motion picture, he has hours—sometimes days. But in a radio drama he may be expected to "fade-out" from one set of circumstances and "fade-in" to another with different emotional adjustments to different people in an entirely different environment, all within two or three seconds. Even the most brilliant actor can't recondition his emotions in such a short space of time.

So what happens? He does the next best thing. Even though he doesn't feel the reality of the lines, he continues. He "indicates" the truth of a scene instead of experiencing and playing it. He can't wait until it comes to him. Dead air is anathema—there must always be sound or new listeners will tune in another station. Constant repetition of this "indicating" or "tricking it" is habit-forming, and it becomes increasingly difficult for the actor to approach his roles any other way. Also, if he works on many different programs, or does a lot of doubling of parts where he has to use different voice registers to get the proper balance with other performers, he develops a bag of voice tricks, which he dishes out to suit script requirements like Western Union with its ready-made telegrams for Mothers' Day.

This requires an efficiency, it's true. Successful radio actors have highly developed techniques. But their performances are, as a rule, only fractionally honest interpretations, by which is meant they have little reality for the performer himself. It's not his fault. Radio constantly demands of him a sacrifice of truth for effect. The listening audience's imagination meets him more than half way. It fills in all the details of a sketchy surface characterization. It requires from him only a partial truth. And any medium that doesn't stimulate him to greater truth, that doesn't encourage a greater creativeness in his work, must necessarily turn a creative actor from growth to retrogression.

My pleasure at seeing my full-page article in *Variety* was mitigated to some degree by a feeling that I was not really entitled to this forum, that I had not yet earned, through accomplishment or experience, the right to address the entire entertainment world.

During the next few days there was much buzzing about the piece among actors with whom I worked in the studios. Many liked it, or said they did; others had points of disagreement. I noted subtle changes in the way most of them related to me. There was an ambivalence—on one hand, a respect for the authority suddenly conferred upon me by *Variety,* and on the other hand an underlying hostility toward the maverick, the befouler of his own nest who had demeaned their profession.

But nothing prepared me for what happened the following Wednesday. I bought a copy of *Variety* at a newsstand, thinking, perhaps, to see a short letter to the editor commenting on my views. (*Organ music in low.*). I leafed casually through the general news, flipped to the motion-picture pages, glancing at different items, until I came to the radio section (*Organ music sting.*) Three full pages of responses, with a bold, boxed, banner headline: RADIO ACTING VERSUS ALL ACTING—SOME REACTIONS TO JOSEPH JULIAN'S PREVIOUS ARTICLE. Agape, I saw column after column of answers from my peers and some of the biggest names in the business. I don't believe *Variety* had ever before or has since devoted so much space to one man's opinion. My name in almost every caption: "THINKS JULIAN SHOULD BE PSYCHOANALYZED"—"AGREES WITH JULIAN, BUT——" "THINKS JULIAN HAS STIMULATED HEALTHY DISCUSSION"—"JULIAN'S ATTITUDE SEEN AS DEFEATISM"—"ACTRESS EXPRESSES SURPRISE AT JULIAN

HOLDING SUCH VIEWS"—"JOE JULIAN'S DARING A SUR-
PRISE"—and many more.

I later learned that this spontaneous outpouring from
professionals across the land was aided and abetted by
Variety's shrewd editor, Robert Landry. He had smelled a
hot controversy and shot off telegrams to notables, not only
of radio but of the theater and film world as well, inviting
their comments. Many responded:

I THRIVE ON RADIO'S BAD CONDITIONS
by Bing Crosby

Hollywood, Jan 21

We have been running the Kraft Music Hall for five years
under the radio principles outlined by Mr. Julian, to wit, quick
readings, short rehearsals and sketchy suggestions of characters, and I'm awfully sorry to say, Julian, old man, that we
haven't lost an actor yet through stagnation. . . .

WHAT PRICE THEAT-AHH
by John Daly

Chicago, Jan 21

Well, wax my mustache and crack my whip, if I haven't just
read an article from the very old school. I had, until this very
moment, been under the obviously wrong impression that
those among our profession who "LIVE THE THEAT-AHH" were
becoming extinct like the fur-collared coats for actors. As one
former spear-carrier to another, I apologize, Mr. Julian, for my
opinions. Surely I have been a traitor to the THEAT-AHH, to as-
sume that such a vulgar thing as making money could be as important as one's art. And to think that I have actually tried at
times, mind you, to get additional work, when had I but read
your article, Mr. Julian, I would surely have realized that I
could not really "live" more than one character at a time.

Funny, the ideas I did have. I had imagined radio acting as a
pretty important and more than that, a damned lucrative field

of work. I have tried in various assignments to interpret the characters honestly and without too much overacting. I had a vague idea that, inasmuch as the audience couldn't see the actors, that possibly the voice might be realized. I confess that I hadn't given a thought to how my artistic ability was being cramped. I guess I just thought myself lucky to have the assignment.

And that horrid thing, the microphone. What a perfectly ducky idea to have a microphone to follow you around. Just imagine being able to snort and bellow from a squatting position, or better still to make love with benefit of davenport. Certainly it would be much more realistic. I shudder to think of how I once played an old prospector, without first finding myself a cave to live in, and then having the mike installed there.

When I think how I've let them "Stagnate my Art" for the sake of a few bucks, I get mad. Who do they think they are? Who knows but what the soul of a Booth or Barrymore lies beneath this rugged chest of mine. And to think I have been sacrificing this great talent to satisfy a lot of vultures who thought they could buy me with filthy money.

I apologize, Mr. Julian, I apologize.

GET THE SCRIPT AHEAD OF TIME AND STUDY
by Irene Rich

Hollywood, Jan 31, 1941

When Mr. Julian said radio drama may lead the actor to artistic stagnation he obviously spoke without knowledge of his subject or the experience to back up what he said. The actor who faces the danger of stagnation in radio is only that actor who lacks the imagination to create his own characters. Radio should not stifle the good actor. It should give him an even greater stimulus to development of his creative faculties. Because in radio we actors must not only create the characters but we must stick to that characterization and maintain it throughout the entire play with no other instrument than the voice.

And that, believe me, is a real test of an actor's imagination and creative powers.

I also take issue with Mr. Julian on what he terms quick reading and short rehearsals. The actor who hasn't the foresight to obtain his script in advance, study it as he would a play script or a scenario, and see himself in relation to the other characters, is not in danger of stagnation. He is already stagnated.

JOE JULIAN'S DARING A SURPRISE

(One established Broadway actress expressed almost complete agreement with Joseph Julian's views. Explaining that she is anxious to get firmly into radio, she asked that her name be withheld.—*Ed.*)

Of course he's right that all an actor can do in radio is to give a surface impression of a part, rather than the full-dimensional characterization possible on the stage. However, I didn't realize the successful radio actors felt that way about it. I just thought I wasn't very good at radio, that my inability to give an immediate performance was limiting my viewpoint. It's comforting to know that one of the best radio actors is dissatisfied with the medium.

DISAGREES WITH JULIAN BUT THINKS HE HAS STIMULATED HEALTHY DISCUSSION

A leading radio actor and director was inclined to pooh-pooh Julian's views in *Variety*, but preferred not to have his name used. In general his attitude was "A radio actor is just selling soap. All that stuff about artistic integrity is the bunk.

"Julian sounds as if he's trying to apply the Stanislavsky method to radio, which would be absurd. If he really believes seriously what he says in that article he must be guilty of outrageous overacting on the air. And I don't believe that's so. I know Joe Julian. He's a good actor."

JULIAN TELLS STORY THAT IS OLD STUFF
By H. Lester Tremayne

Mr. Julian's article is not new, unusual nor different. It sums up rather disconnectedly the constant griping which I have heard every day of my life in radio for the last ten years. For every fault relative to radio acting there is a comparable fault in stage or picture work. There is also an opposite or constructive angle to each of Mr. Julian's list of radio faults.

Radio is a new medium which has its own peculiarities and technique. Any actor who goes into radio seriously should expect to make the adjustments necessary to a business which in its very mechanics is completely different from any acting form heretofore. If he is not able to make these adjustments, if he feels his artistic integrity will be jeopardized, he should certainly take his integrity, which no doubt is of the hothouse variety, where conditions will promote its growth.

JULIAN'S ATTITUDE SEEN AS DEFEATISM
By Katharine Seymour

As a writer who listens to radio drama professionally and critically, I can say in all honesty that I am constantly amazed at the excellent performances of radio actors—performances which rarely betray the brief rehearsal periods of which Mr. Julian complains. Perhaps he is overly self critical and modest. After all, capable artists of integrity in any field are rarely satisfied with their own performances.

As a general criticism, it seems to me that the tone of Mr. Julian's article is strictly defeatist, and it is this very attitude which has helped retard the growth of radio as an entertainment form. Writers, like actors, are irked at times by the limitations of the medium. We, too, would like to indicate significant bits of business instead of depending entirely upon dialogue or sound effects. But most of us feel that it's futile to brood over radio's limitations. Instead, we face the challenge of the medium and find satisfaction when we succeed in creating a mood through the only props at our disposal, sound effects and music.

RADIO IS BRUTAL BUT A CHALLENGE
by Janet Logan

Chicago, Jan 21, 1941

So radio ruins actors—well, perhaps it does—some of them. But radio gives opportunities and offers challenges which no sincere actor can question. The very limitations of radio provide a test. Without makeup—without scenery—without the inspiration of a visible audience, the player must develop a living, breathing human being.

Dials can be twisted so easily that the drama wherein the acting consists of a few "mike tricks" would soon be in Limbo. The public's not stupid nor too easily fooled.

SYMPATHIZES, BUT PICTURE TOO BLACK
By Hugh Studebaker

Chicago, Jan 21, 1941

While I'm inclined to sympathize with Julian's viewpoint, I can not agree that the picture is quite so black. This is due, perhaps to the mellowness—or resignation, induced by fourteen years spent in our puzzling and catch-as-catch-can art form. We've come a long way, developing our little bag of tricks, which is so necessary to bring to life several characters daily. And now we have come to the days of the Corwins and the Obolers. And we find, strangely, that out of the ruck something good has been emerging which I sincerely believe will ultimately bring satisfaction to the groping heart of the actor. Considering the extent to which experimentation in the baby field of radio acting has been limited by the necessary priority of the commercial, I can't help thinking that a great deal has been achieved. Whether we shall ever capture the high moments of elation for which we love the theater, so long as it remains necessary to watch the director, listen for sound, and hope to God our pages aren't mixed, I don't profess to know. At least it's a challenge!

A RADIO PERFORMANCE REQUIRES INTELLECTUAL TOTALITARIANISM
By Albert N. Williams
Casting Director, NBC, New York

Yes, Joe Julian is right when he states that radio is the director's medium rather than the actor's. He is as right as a musician might be in proposing that symphonic is a conductor's medium rather than an instrumentalist's. To most radio actors, and the following remark holds true for radio writers, directors, in fact, most people connected with the industry, radio still appears to be merely a broadcast version of theater.

Radio is no more theater than theater is Greek Festive dance—they are successive derivatives of each other. While it can never be denied that the ideal training ground for an actor is the legitimate stage, the actor, once trained, must, like the novice pilot, resort to different maneuvers when on the air. . . .

Radio, in itself, is not an art. The sound of voice is not an art. The sound of music is not an art. The sound of a streetcar is not an art. Radio is only an electrical means of transmission of sound from a studio into the homes of the listeners. The art lies in the nearness to reality of the total sound, as mixed inside a control room. Most artistic effort is based on the assumption that all mental instruments can act simultaneously toward a perception of truth. Only one of these instruments is employed in listening to radio—the ear. Therefore, all adventures before the microphone must be submissive to the entire. Radio, more than any other of the arts, requires of its citizens an intellectual totalitarianism. Any coloration requires that that factor serve as a north star for the others. In the theater it is the simulation of living people. In films it is the God-sense of being able to oversee all. In radio, since sound can only be real in so far as it has meaning, the words themselves rather than the vibrancy of their delivery will be valid.

It is that nature of radio which must be understood, and which understanding will do away with much artistic unhappiness. When actors understand the microphone, they will no longer resent it, and it will not appear brutal to them. True, sound is one-dimensional, but good performances can also be one-dimensional.

Radio is the art form of intimacy. Into people's homes, not a theater, is the ultimate direction of a show. Would one increase credibility in a living room with gestures, stage waits, smiles, handkerchief gymnastics?

As for the emotional jerkiness resulting from radio's rapid scene changes, we sometime expect our musicians to dive from a ponderous adagio into a delicate scherzo in the course of one beat. . . . Radio will always demand a sacrifice of truth for effect. Effect is the basis of all emotional and intellectual impact, and only by proving that it exerts those impacts does radio justify itself as a cultural factor of modern life.

It all boils down to the fact that while radio is a challenge for actors, it actually demands very little acting in the Broadway sense of the word. It demands careful and studied interpretation of the words of the script in order that the meaning of the words may be etched on the listener's mind. . . . The shut-in, the invalid, the isolated person wants human communication rather than the thrilling dissonance of pent-up artistic ecstasies. For actors to resent radio is unnecessary, and creates a temperamental disaffection which has unfortunate results. They will not resent it when they understand more clearly the nature of their medium.

DIRECTOR COMMENTS
By George Zachary
(Director of the Andre Kostelanetz program and the Campbell Playhouse)

It's perfectly true the radio actor lacks the opportunity for development he would have in the theater, but his whole performance has a different purpose and perspective. . . . I know of no radio actors whose performances improve perceptibly with rehearsal. If a regular radio actor doesn't get a characterization right with the first reading, there's no use trying to change him, I know I'm in a hole, but I generally expect a bad first reading from a stage actor, and it doesn't worry me. I know he has to grow in the part and it will be much better in performance. But radio actors are vastly superior to stage actors in radio-acting technique. Radio has developed the most versatile group of actors ever known to the entertainment field! . . . Julian speaks of the impossibility of an actor making mood transitions in a few seconds. Joe himself makes those transitions, but both Joe and the listener need help. That's where music can be important. A few notes of the proper atmospheric music will bring both the actor and listener into a totally different mood in two or three seconds. In some ways that can give added emphasis to a scene. In general, I think Julian's opinions are thoughtful and sound.

NO NEED FOR ACTOR "FRUSTRATION"
By Erick Barnouw

Dear Joe Julian:
The artistic frustration of most radio actors I wouldn't want to deny, but I feel you're wrong to blame it on your medium.

You bewail the "cold unresponsive microphone." Does a novelist get peeved at his typewriter for not chuckling at his jokes? It just happens that novelists and radio actors don't have the privilege of witnessing the artistic experiences they provide their audiences. This is part of the nature of these and many other arts, and simply offers an extra challenge to the imagination. In these fields the artist has to be more, not less, of an artist.

You feel frustrated because you can't do gestures and "bits of business." You feel this makes radio acting "incomplete." But one of the most gratifying of arts, cartooning, is exciting precisely because of its incompleteness. The less it tells and shows, the more it merely suggests, the better we like it. A window-dummy is more "complete," but hardly provides artist or audience with more gratification. Radio acting also works in suggestion, not demonstration, some actors prefer it for this.

You bemoan having to act by the clock. Every art has mechanical strictures, and the real artist not only accepts but often welcomes them. For centuries poets have kept busy at sonnets, with just fourteen lines and a torturing rhyme-scheme, when they could just as well write loose odes. Working within imposed limits is part of the gratification of any art. What's wrong with fourteeen minutes?

You feel it's hard to keep your imagination clear in the presence of mikes, scripts, clocks and directors behind aquarium windows. Is a painter distracted by his easels and his bottles? You seem to miss real tables, chairs, doors and other literal paraphernalia. Does a poet have to sit in the woods to write about birds? It isn't just high-hat to compare radio acting with painting, poetry, novel-writing. These all bank heavily on the imagination of both artist and audience, and are challenging and gratifying for that reason.

Then why do radio actors feel frustrated? Because, as you say, writers give you chiefly drivel to act—which they do because producers buy chiefly drivel—which they do because audiences seem to cling to drivel—which they do because they've been conditioned, by film, magazines and radio, to drivel. That vicious circle, in spite of occasional exciting flurries of better writing, makes for progressive deterioration. In a time of precarious profits that's also true of shoes, and shirts and mayonnaise. That's what frustrates you, not your medium. Incidentally, I often hear your excellent acting.

RADIO TOUGH ON NEWCOMERS

San Francisco, Jan 21

Joseph Julian's dictum, as expressed in last week's *Variety*, that the nature of radio leads actors down the road to artistic stagnation, draws a divvy here. Some agree with the New Yorker's contention while others concede the point that ether drama is largely a director's medium. Representative comments follow:

Phil Stearns (seventeen years experience as actor, director, producer on radio, stage, screen): "Julian is about half right, although the medium hasn't even been scratched as yet. I don't agree with him on characterization—a good actor can take a good script and build a character that will be remembered. Orson Welles has proven that. Julian is right when he says radio actors tend to drift into artistic stagnation, but it is not the fault of radio acting. A microphone performer who takes his work seriously can make himself stand out on the air just as in the theater."

Helen Morgan (stage, radio writing background): "Julian is partly right; not only in acting, but in writing and producing, radio is always under the gun, which accounts for a lot of the sloppy drama on the air. When it becomes financially possible to give players sufficient rehearsal time, radio acting will improve. But someday there must be more of a closed-door in radio acting. Today, anybody who can read writing is considered capable of acting on the air—it's still too much like a great big amateur show. When they start limiting radio drama to people with real microphone ability, things will improve. Radio has been made too easy."

Zella Layne (*Dr. Kate* serial): "It's a matter of becoming a topflight reader more than anything else. The script writer has the best chance. A radio actor hasn't much chance to do anything but do a good job of reading at sight."

Jeanne Bate (NBC actress): "In most radio shows today

you're not acting—you're helping to sell a product. Furthermore, in daytime shows you're playing to people who are doing something else while they're listening and wouldn't know a characterization if they heard one because they aren't paying enough attention. That is reserved for the big programs at night."

Jack Kirkwood (with a lifetime in the theater behind him): "Yeah—hard work and experience—IN THE THEATRE. This bird Joseph Julian knows what he is talking about. Radio hasn't developed ten real actors in its history—all the good ones came from the stage. Radio is worse than the picture business for new actors; all a guy can do is just what the director tells him. That's been my squawk for years. There isn't a chance for a newcomer to start in radio and get anywhere. Joseph knows his oats."

I was overwhelmed by this extraordinary burst of publicity, and fearful it would spell the end of my burgeoning livelihood. After all, if radio did such horrible things to actors, why would I want to work in such a corroding medium? Why should directors even bother to call me?

I went to the *Variety* office and confided my fears to editor Landry, who assured me I couldn't buy publicity like that for $50,000, and predicted I would soon be busier than ever. The following week he published more letters in reaction to my piece—some pro, some con—from Gene Autry, Conrad Nagel, Chester Lauck of *Lum and Abner,* and many more. But since practically none addressed itself to my main point, I decided an answer to the answers was in order. I wrote a "clarifying" piece for the next issue.

JOE JULIAN IN GENTLE REPLY TO HIS CRITICS

New York, Jan 29, '41

Editor, *Variety*

I seemed to have opened Pandora's box—or something. While most of the reactions to my *Variety* article entirely disregarded my basic premise, I found them interesting because they illuminate the general confusion that exists on the entire subject of radio acting—in fact, all acting.

However, the general tone of the replies tend to give an impression that I wrote the article in a white heat of anger or disgust with radio, as such. One of the comments even referred to my "daring" in risking the resentment of agency executives and directors by openly stating my views. I would like to clear up any such misconception. In the first place, the radio industry provides me with quite a decent living, and anyone who doesn't have a healthy respect for his means of livelihood is either an idiot or a professional iconoclast. About risking the resentment of directors, I didn't think in those terms. I assumed, I suppose, they would accept it as intended, not as destructive criticism, but an attempt at a purely objective analysis and comparison of the creative possibilities of actors in radio in relation to the other entertainment fields.

I recognize the validity of radio itself as a wonderful new art form, but not radio acting. Acting is the art form, not radio acting or stage acting or film acting. The actor's approach to his part is the same in all three mediums. His tools are basically the same. He uses his emotions, personal experience, his powers of concentration, imagination, observation, his voice and his body. Even in radio he uses his body. He unconsciously twists, turns, and gestures within the confines of the mike "beam," because his main function is to create out of his material the greatest possible reality for himself, not his audience. If he believes what he is acting, the audience believes. And this is true of acting in any medium. But in radio there are more mechanical strictures and distractions to prevent his building this reality for himself, than in other acting fields. Therefore in radio he has less opportunity to use his creative energies. One of my knuckle rappers considers this a healthy challenge. True, the lack of real contact with his fellow performers stimulates the radio actor's imagination to a certain extent. He must dig deeper down into himself for the emotions that would flow more naturally from proper adjustment to his co-actors. But this virtue, I believe, is more than offset by developing in the actor a tendency toward an introverted kind of acting that can become artistically as unhealthy as can an introverted way of living.

And the distractions of holding scripts, finding the next line, watching directors for cues, etc. Are these healthy challenges? Do they make an actor sharpen his powers of concentration? Then why not sharpen them sharper by bringing even more distractions into the studio? Maybe a little man could be hired to run around the studio distracting the actors—making funny faces at them while they're on the air.

Erik Barnouw makes the point that "for centuries poets have kept busy at sonnets with just fourteen lines and a torturing rhyme-scheme, when they could just as well write loose odes. Working within imposed limits is part of the gratification of any art."

The poets who turned to sonnets didn't impose these restrictions on themselves for the gratification they got out of overcoming handicaps. In all progressive art, form is derived from content. One doesn't arbitrarily select a form then fill it in with stuff. The stuff determines the form it needs. The poets wrote sonnets because to them it was the best way of expressing a particular poetic concept.

But the radio actor doesn't select radio acting because it's a better method of expression for him than the stage. Usually it's because it gives him a much better living.

I'm strongly tempted to argue other points made by your correspondents. I feel much good can come of a pro and con discussion of the subject, even if it only makes for a greater awareness in actors of the tools of their trade (a long step towards using them better), but I am a little afraid that prolonging the argument might lay my motives open to question. You know— actor—publicity, etc.??? So— I better gather up all my split infinitives and dangling participles and run along. I'm late for rehearsal.

                                                            Joseph Julian.

For months the articles were the subject of discussion and argument around the studios, ad agencies, and cocktail parties, with enough support for my thesis for my name to acquire some prestige as a serious, thoughtful actor.

I was especially pleased to get a call from Montgomery Clift, a rising young actor whose work I greatly admired, and with whom I had, in some way, felt a kinship. We met at Colbee's Restaurant, a hangout for radio people in the old CBS Building at 485 Madison Avenue, where he told me he had wanted to meet me because I had exactly expressed his own feelings about the whole radio acting phenomenon.

I began getting calls for jobs from directors I had never met. Landry's prophecy was fulfilled. Ironically, after writing on the deleterious effect of radio on creative actors, I became busier than ever.

5. "Michael West" and After

Sometime in mid-1941 I ran into Larry Menkin, who had been my roommate at WLW, and later became one of radio's most prolific writers—*Famous Jury Trials, Mollé Mystery Theater, Harlem Detective*, and hundreds more. He was now freelancing in New York. He informed me that my friend Thomas Ashwell was no longer at WLW. On the strength of his job there as program manager, he had talked himself into becoming general manager of WXYZ in Detroit. Another step up the ladder. I wondered if he was using the same system.

My own progress was greatly aided in 1941 by a Greenwich Village neighbor, Julian Funt, who was writing a soap opera that had been on the air for five years called *Big Sister*. For some reason I brought out the big brother in him. He always showed a warm interest in my activities and welfare, and we became friends.

He had a habit of closely questioning people about themselves and mutual acquaintances. But as I got to know him better, I realized that it was out of a healthy human concern, and that an appetite for the intimate details of peoples' lives was part of a good writer's basic equipment. In fact, I began to envy his energetic curiosity and tried to cultivate more of it in myself as I realized its application to my own profession.

I was also not unaware of his writer's interest in me as a character—which, perhaps, I was (am?). In any case, when I met Funt, I had not yet found my center of gravity; my feet were planted firmly in the sky, and I collected folk songs—attributes of a role he wrote into the story line of *Big Sister*. It came out as Michael West, rootless, embittered young wanderer who sang folk songs and accompanied himself on the guitar. In the program, Michael falls under the influence of Big Sister, who eases his pain and restores his faith in people. Since I had inspired the character, a little neighborly nepotism seemed in order. Funt got me an audition and, I suspect, used his influence to help me get the part.

The role had such a successful listener response that after several months the sponsor, Lever Brothers, decided to do a spinoff and give Michael West his own show. Now that Michael was to be the lead, it was decided—and this was typical of sponsor madness—that general auditions should be held for the role. I was invited to compete. Perhaps, now that it was a starring role, with a contract and more money involved, they wanted to be sure they couldn't do better. Whatever their reasons, I again won the part. They called the show *Bright Horizon, the Story of Michael West*. In a way, it was a complete reversal of the normal daytime formula. It had a hero instead of the usual heroine, and a woman announcer instead of a man. And, for good measure, a Miss Ora Nichols worked the sound effects—the only woman on CBS who handled sound.

The new show got off to a good start. In those days, considerable newspaper and magazine space was devoted to radio, and radio reviews were as widespread as are those of plays and films today. This was Hobe Morrison's *Variety* coverage:

Bright Horizon
Serial
With Joseph Julian, Alice Frost, Santos Ortega, Sid Slon, Chester Stratton, Marjorie Anderson, John Gart.
15 Mins.
Lever Bros.
Mon–Fri., 11:30 A.M.
(Young & Rubicam)

Lever Bros. appears to have a lively bet in this show, based on the Michael West character formerly part of the *Big Sister* series. Format of the show is a change from standard serials, while the West character is unusual and meaty. Because the story is obviously going to get a completely new slant so as to steer it away from the *Big Sister* plot, it's difficult to predict how good the yarn may be, but on the basis of Monday's (25) debut, *Bright Horizon* has definite prospects.

Full title of the program is *Bright Horizon, the Story of Michael West*. Takes the form of a first-person narrative by the hero, a soft-hearted idealistic guy beneath the surface of hard-bitten disillusionment. Narrative fades quickly into dramatization, but cuts back for brief first-person narration to afford scene changes. Most of the initial episode was flashback to familiarize the listeners with the story's characters, situation and background. It was neatly telescoped, however, thereby quickly preparing to cut loose from its *Big Sister* source and embark on a story line of its own. Characters, all but Michael, apparently slated to fade from future scripts, are sharp, particularly the hero. Dialogue is good.

Production, direction and performance on the opener were

excellent. Pacing and mood were nicely handled. Joseph Julian had the proper blend of bitterness and romantic softness as the hero, while Alice Frost was expressive and authoritative as Ruth Wayne, the title part of Big Sister, and set to fade from *Horizon* pronto. Santos Ortega, Sidney Slon and Chester Stratton were also convincing in supporting roles. John Gart's organ bridges and cues were notably helpful.

Balancing the presence of a man as the central character, Marjorie Anderson, instead of a male announcer, reads the intros and commercials. It's a welcome variation, besides which she handles the blurbs rather persuasively. Product on the regular 11:30 A.M. show is Swan Soap, while on the 2 P.M. repeat to the coast it's Lipton's tea.

Hobe.

Having my first lead in a radio series upped me considerably in my own esteem. But Bobby Gibson and his busy little manager tried to swipe some of my glory. Since I couldn't sing, the producers hired this . . . this baritone, to be my singing voice when the occasion demanded. Naturally, to him the singing was more important than the acting; therefore, Michael West was played by Bobby Gibson the singer, not Joe Julian the actor. Every day the busy little manager would grab all the fan mail and answer requests for a photograph of Michael West by sending an autographed picture of his client.

The papers had some fun with it, too. Ben Kaplan, in his nationally syndicated column, "For the Love of Mike," wrote:

> When Michael sings, a teardrop springs
>   From optics feminine.
> When he emotes, each maiden notes
>   The melody within;
> But in their bliss the hearers miss
>   A most important fact:

> Two not alike play role of "Mike,"
> One sings and one does act.

The problem of who was really Michael West was resolved six months later: we were both fired, and replaced by Richard Kollmar, who could both sing and act.

It hurt. I tried to console myself that I was let go to save a salary, but I didn't believe myself. Actors don't accept reasons like that. They convince themselves they gave a terrible performance, that they lost whatever talent they had, that there is no hope and they will never work again. As I said, actors do not generally have strong egos. Mine shrank to nothing. I sulked, unable to bring myself to face other actors, or look for work. Having been to Olympus, how could I go back to making the rounds?

My misery was mitigated when one day I got a call for a running part on *The O'Neills*, a daily serial about a poor Irish family. But that didn't last long. After a few months I wound up in "jail," an innocent victim of the melodramatic plot line—typical of *The O'Neills*—and a major reason it failed in its attempt to become the Irish counterpart of *The Goldbergs*, an enormously successful family story, which had been running since 1929, that is, for twelve years. But the Goldbergs couldn't be duplicated because there was no duplicate for Gertrude Berg, who wrote it and played the leading role of Molly. Gertrude was one of radio's jewels. A middle-aged housewife who had never written in her life, she decided she didn't have enough to do, with only a husband and growing children to take care of. She therefore conceived the idea for a serial about a poor Jewish family in New York, wrote a few episodes, and sent them to NBC. They bought it. And bought her as writer and star. It was not melodramatic, nor was it a typical soap opera of suffering virtue and *Sturm und Drang,* but rather a cozy comedy of small human foibles that nearly everyone could identify with. Gertrude Berg created one of the most famous characters in the history of radio—a Jewish mama who was not smothering or abrasive, but warm, sensitive, and amusing. With no professional background, she wrote and played with a perfect ear for the nuances of Jewish speech and character. Her "Yoo hoo! Is anybody?" as she called to her upstairs neighbor was but one of hundreds. And you didn't have to be Jewish to love Gertrude. With an audience of millions, she probably did more, five times a week for over two decades, to combat anti-Semitism than any individual in history.

At one time, after about eight or nine years, NBC decided *The Goldbergs* had been on the air long enough, and announced its cancellation. Outraged listeners howled their protest in a storm of letters. NBC bowed to *vox populi.*

6. Corwin

Much of the nostalgia for old-time radio relates to the fun of being horrified by *Inner Sanctum, Lights Out,* and *The Shadow.* Or laughing, without guilt, at the ethnic humor of *Moran and Mack (The Two Black Crows)* and *Amos 'n' Andy;* or crying along with the soap-opera queens; or giving your mind over to the wild science-fiction tales of *Dimension X* and *Two Thousand Plus.*

There were also interesting realistic dramas. Shows such as the *Lux Radio Theater,* directed and hosted by Cecil B. DeMille, featured movie stars in radio adaptations of famous motion pictures. *Cavalcade of America* presented weekly dramatizations of American history. Sponsored by Du Pont, the series paid $150 per script, for which they could get good authors such as the poet Norman Rosten and the playwright-to-be, Arthur Miller.

But some of us fondly remember radio for its richer cultural nourishment—for its achievements on the level of art. And there were quite a few. Many, if not most, were created by Norman Corwin.

There were early experimental programs like *The Columbia Workshop* and *Studio One*, where a few imaginative writers and directors like Irving Reis, William Robson, Marc Blitzstein, Earle McGill, and Charles Martin tried out new techniques with sometimes interesting results. But no one stretched radio's horizons as did Norman Corwin.

A newspaperman for the first ten years of his professional career, Corwin went to work for CBS in 1938 and quickly grasped the fundamentals of this new medium. Without any real apprenticeship or theater background, he began to write, produce, and direct radio shows. The technology of radio excited him, and he immediately began to explore its possibilities. He had an intuitive understanding of how to deal with performers (fragile creatures that we are), a love of words, a poetic thrust, an orderly mind, a scientific curiosity, a social conscience, a delightful sense of humor, and a soaring imagination—all reflected in his plays.

He pioneered new techniques in mixing sound effects and developed original production devices, while writing an astonishing number and variety of comedies and dramas that ranged from his charming fantasy *My Client Curley*—the story of a little boy who owned a caterpillar that could dance only to the tune of "Yes Sir, That's My Baby"—to *On a Note of Triumph*, his eloquent and powerful punctuation to the climax of World War II; from *Mary and the Fairy*, a whimsical satire about a lonely lady stuffing her empty life with the dreams society thrusts upon her, to "We Hold These Truths," a moving, poetic documentation of the evolution of the Bill of Rights.

Many of Corwin's works had considerable social impact. "We Hold These Truths," for instance, planted its statement in the ears of more people than any other single dramatic performance in history.

It was a special hour program, written at the request of the Office of Facts and Figures in Washington, to celebrate the 150th Anniversary of the Bill of Rights. Produced in Hollywood, on December 15, 1941, portions of it originated in New York and Washington. Bernard Herrmann composed a special score for the dramatic sequences, conducting a symphony orchestra in the Hollywood studio, while Leopold Stokowski led the New York Philharmonic Orchestra from New York in the national anthem. The program was carried over all four major networks in prime time, and concluded with an address to the nation by Franklin D. Roosevelt. The Crossley reports (the main rating poll of the time) estimated the number of listeners at over sixty million! And what a cast: Lionel Barrymore, Edward Arnold, Walter Brennan, Bob Burns, Walter Huston, Marjorie Main, Edward G. Robinson, James Stewart, Rudy Vallee, Orson Welles and . . . the President of the United States.

Corwin stimulated a number of other fine American writers to write for the medium. Archibald MacLeish developed *The Fall of the City*, a long, dramatic allegory about Hitler and man's lust to be enslaved. With Corwin's encouragement, Maxwell Anderson and Stephen Vincent Benét came up with several poetic dramas. Millard Lampell write a touching elegy for Abraham Lincoln, called *The Lonesome Train*. All of these were directed and given a special radio life by Corwin. But, with the exception of the Lincoln funeral story, where music and the mournful train whistle played an important part, they would have been as effective read in a book or presented on a stage— as would have countless other presentations adapted from poems, dramas, short stories and novels.

But Corwin was pure radio. A word and sound man; a music and effects man, who conceived in those terms— abundantly. As Clifton Fadiman wrote:

> Corwin is so much the technician that he conducts public ex- periments with his medium, coaxes it to perform tricks, plays with it, treats it with the eager curiosity of a boy with his first chemical set. What is important about him, beyond his mastery of his medium, is that he has something to say, and a heart and a mind with which to say it. His masterpiece, "We Hold These Truths," provides irrefutable evidence of his ability to manipu- late actors, words, machines, and ether waves, so that the com- bination expresses clear, lofty, and inspiring thought.*

Carl Van Doren wrote that, "Corwin was to radio what Marlowe was to the Elizabethan stage." But in terms of sheer prolificacy, I know of no peer on his level of achievement. In 1941 he committed himself to the colossal task of writing, producing, and directing for twenty-six consecutive weeks a special CBS series, *Twenty-six by Corwin*, which won him an American Writer's Congress Award. In a foreword to the published version, he wrote:

> Each of these plays was written against a deadline, and most of them within a week's time. A schedule of this sort is dangerous and should be tried only once in the lifetime of a conscientious radiowright. I gave up all but a few distractions and placed a

* From the Introduction to *More by Corwin: 16 Radio Dramas by Nor- man Corwin*. New York. Henry Holt & Co., 1944.

strict limit on working hours: never more than twenty-four in a day.

He also wrote production notes for these plays which provide an insight into his creative process: the hard work, the careful casting, the long experimentation to achieve precise effects.

The first of the twenty-six was "The Odyssey of Runyon Jones," a fantasy about a little boy's search for his dog, Pootzy, who had died and been sent to Curgatory. On the way, he encountered Father Time, Mother Nature, her assistant Blossom, a Giant, and many other fantasy characters. Here are some of Corwin's notes on that production:

CASTING:
Without a sensitive and versatile Runyon, you might as well all go home. He should be between nine and twelve, and sound earnest, purposeful, persistent. Don't, under any circumstances, employ a Runyon who sounds fresh or oversmart or whining. So many radio kids sound that way, although as a class they are better than the horrible Hollywood junior brigade.

Father Time must, of course, be old to be credible. The character should justify the "crackpot" comment which is made later by the Chairman of the Board of Curgatory.

Mother Nature is a busy but not overbearing executive type: the efficient controller of all things natural; the kindly helper; the disciplinarian. M.N.'s assistant, Blossom, is a silly child.

The Giant is a stock giant. Arthur Vinton played him with humor and vitality, deepening an already deep voice, and rolling his speech in a wondrous way.

ACTING:
Everybody whom Runyon meets in his travels treats him as an adult, never as a child. Nobody wastes sympathy, except perhaps the Superintendent, who is aware of the boy's unusual at-

tachment to his dog. Father Time is too daft to care much; Mother Nature is accustomed to all kinds of strange petitions; the Giant has worries of his own; the personnel of Curgatory is polite but firm, always addressing the boy as "Jones." None of the characters should be travestied.

SOUND:

The only problem is that of the background for the Father Time sequence. I found that the best effect was achieved by slowing down a recording of a cuckoo clock. At normal speed this effect was a pleasant "ding," followed by a cheerful "cuckoo," but I reduced it to a speed so low that the ding became a tremendous and deep-chested "BONG," and the optimistic chirrup of the cuckoo became a lugubrious two-note wail of a melancholy whistling buoy. This succeeded somehow in creating an effect of great space, of mysterious gyrations, of the weird inner workings of the solar system.

REHEARSAL ROUTINE:

The chief production worries are the blending of sound, music, and speech in the Time Sequence and the interview between the Giant and Runyon. The former can best be accomplished by using a separate microphone for each element, being careful not to allow the background of sound to override speech. This scene will be soupy unless one works hard to maintain clear perspectives.

In the Giant scene, complete isolation is necessary if Runyon is to sound small and the Giant big. I placed Runyon in a dead booth * and reduced the level of his microphone on the control board, while the Giant had the whole studio to himself, and an echo chamber to boot.

---

* A dead booth is a booth made of portable walls, which is set up within a studio to isolate an actor from sound or music. In effect, it serves as a studio-within-a-studio. A microphone placed within a booth is easily controlled by the engineer, so that the voice of the actor is not drowned out by heavy sound effects or music coming from the studio proper. The principle of the booth is an important one in production, and is almost indispensable in the handling of complicated setups.

Corwin published these production notes for the guidance of directors of future productions, of which I am sure there have been very few—for the simple reason that, outside of the networks, not many stations have the staff, talent, or facilities for such productions. And if Corwin was thinking of the glorious future, well, the glorious future has arrived, and good radio drama is in the middle of a long death. The small but rich body of radio literature, which he brought so lovingly to life, lies languishing in a few libraries and second-hand book shops, under the titles *Thirteen By Corwin* and *More By Corwin*—a great shame and deprivation for the present generation!

The publicity surrounding the *Variety* articles had brought me to Corwin's attention. It was the beginning of the most rewarding relationship of my career. He began casting me in bit parts in some of his "Twenty-six" series—including "The Odyssey of Runyon Jones." The final scene of that play was, for me, one of radio's wonderful moments. The bureaucrats of Curgatory had finally granted Jones permission to see his dog. We hear the ponderous footsteps of a guard (me) echoing down a long marble corridor, contrasting with the tiny, rapid steps of the boy. The suspense is heightened by continuing the footsteps an inordinate length of time. Finally they stop. The guard says, "Here we are. He's right inside that door." Runyon, barely able to control his voice, says, "He's right inside there?" "Yes," says the guard, "just open the door and walk right in." There is a pause. "What's the matter?" asks the guard. There is another silence, and the little boy asks, plaintively, "Do I look all right?" "Oh, yes, Mr. Jones," the guard replies. We hear the sound of a doorknob turning and the beginning of a door opening—then a dissolve into music.

I landed my first lead in a Corwin play in the summer of 1942, a segment of his monumental *This Is War* series, entitled, "To the Young." A large percentage of his work now dealt with World War II and its issues, and *This Is War* was an umbrella title for a number of special hour programs carried simultaneously over all the networks. Some segments were written by various authors, but all were produced and directed by Corwin. This is how *Variety* reviewed "To the Young."

This Is War No. 11
With Joseph Julian
Saturday, 7 P.M.
All Networks

Other chapters have been more cohesively knit as to framework, but "To the Young" proved as dynamic a document as anything that has preceded it on this series. It presented the case against the Nazi foe not through virulent name-calling, but through citations from factual data showing the depths of degradation into which Nazi child education and cultural life has sunk. It preached unity and faith in our allies by relating the heroic exploits of the British, Russians, and the Chinese. It piled into our own sixth column with a singeing scorn, quoting their undermining cant and at one point categorizing them with the crack, "There's a crackpot market for anything that's anti-sensible and anti-decent."

Joseph Julian . . . was posed as a young member of our armed forces who meets a Cockney flier, a Russian guerilla, a German soldier who, once a member of his country's underground movement had, when the opportunity offered, deserted to the Soviet side, and a young, college-bred woman from the Chinese auxiliary forces. He learns in his travels that the "cranks and some editors" at home have been lying to him about the Reds, that there is a method to their stirring up of anti-British sentiment and that the accent is not only on youth but on victory.

Johnny Green's was a competent bit of scoring.

Odec.

In those days, such strongly political programs did not bring down the wrath of the FCC on the networks, or a clamor for equal time by "responsible opposing views," as it would today, because on the war issue there was no real gap either between the major political parties or between government and the people.

By this time most Americans had committed their hearts and muscle to the war against Hitler, and sentiment was growing for the United States to open a second front in Europe to relieve the pressure on England, whose cities were being blasted day and night.

There was scarcely a factory in Detroit that was not turning out something for England. And in California the air was so heavy with war planes being tested near aircraft factories, and causing such unrelenting noise, that Hollywood studios had to rewrite scripts to eliminate outdoor shooting locations. With the exception of fringe groups, Americans supported decisions to send these massive supplies, because intuitively they understood that the war was pro-humanity and that Britain was fighting our battle, too.

Landing the lead in "To The Young" was a fateful bit of casting for me. My performance of a soldier going off to war would be directly responsible for plunking me down in the midst of a real war only two weeks later.

In the middle of July, 1942, I received a call from Paul

White, head of CBS News. Would I be interested in flying to London within the next few days to play the lead in a special six-week series called *An American in England* that Norman Corwin was doing from the BBC, a series that was to be shortwaved back to America? Apparently Corwin, who was already in London, had intended to use Burgess Meredith as the star, but there had been some last-minute trouble getting the army to release him. Remembering my *To the Young* performance, Corwin cabled CBS to fly me over.

Would I be interested? I practically flew over to CBS to sign the contract. It didn't even occur to me to bargain over my fee; the paper they pushed at me stated: "We will pay you the sum of Two Hundred and Fifty Dollars per program on which you render your services." Out of that I had to pay my own living expenses. For starring in an important, international Corwin series to be heard throughout the British Isles and America, the salary had to be an all-time low. I've always been a soft-nosed businessman; the hot, tumbling visions of a trip to England at war must have softened my brain, too. I signed.

CBS expeditiously arranged my passport and papers, and three days later I was on a train speeding toward the Canadian border. In my pocket was a sealed envelope of instructions, not to be opened until I arrived in Montreal. All I was told was that I would be flying the Atlantic in one of the bombers being ferried from American factories to the Royal Air Force in England; and the time and place of the departures were highly secret.

As the train ploughed through the night, my thoughts and feelings came fast and furious: I had never flown the

Atlantic before—in fact, very few other people had. I had never been to England, and here I was on my way to an England that was being blasted into rubble. War—till then an abstraction—was about to become a reality. And, professionally, new horizons were opening for me: soon I would be performing in most living rooms of the United States and the British Isles. Before I had left New York, there had already been considerable publicity about Corwin having selected me for this choice assignment.

I played games to calm myself. An actor's self-hypnosis. "I'm going on a weekend pleasure trip; I'll be back Sunday night." The pitch blackness outside the train window was suddenly shattered by a concentration of thousands of lights: a defense plant night shift, working full blast. Reality. This was no weekend pleasure trip. I was on my way to a close-up of history and horror.

Jottings from my journal:

July 23, 1942: Montreal! A busy, bustling city. Oldness and war in the air. A mélange of accents and uniforms. I've become a foreigner. Streets dense with RAF fliers snapping salutes at passing superiors. Opened my sealed orders. There was a phone number to call and identify myself as 537. Male voice told me to wait there. Within fifteen minutes a limousine picked me up and drove me to the airport, where I was fitted with an oxygen mask, parachute, and shown a film about what to do if the pilot has to "ditch" in the ocean. It brought out the coward in me! Can such things happen? We're to leave at 9:30 in the morning.

July 24, 1942: Flight cancelled. Bad weather. Prospect of another day of nail-gnawing too much. Saw movie tonight: *This Above All*, about the bombing of London. Shocked into realization I'm on my way to all that. Hope we're not cancelled tomorrow. Corwin must be terribly worried. This is Friday, the series starts Monday! And I haven't rehearsed, or even seen the script!

July 25: We've been in the air ten minutes. Can't take my nose from the window. Five other passengers dozing or reading. Amazed at their relaxation. Only at takeoff was there a surge of feeling. Spontaneously, everyone looked at everyone, grinned, and gave "thumbs up." Maybe they're at ease because this is only the overland part of the flight. Must be climbing, I'm getting cold. Just had a shock. Three corks shot up at me from thermos bottles. [There was no pressurization in those days.] We've hit a rain and hail storm. Everyone is nervously fingering the straps of his parachute. They all yell, "Sit down!" as a young Frenchman stands up to stretch and touches the defroster pipe that runs along the ceiling. Seems "icing up" is feared most by pilots on this run.

Just landed at Gander, Newfoundland airport, biggest in the world. Carved smack out of the wilderness. A wilderness of lakes kept apart by crazy strips of land for hundreds of miles. Three administrations here. Royal Canadian Air Force, American Air Force, and the British Ferry Command. Anti-aircraft guns bristling everywhere. Terrific traffic. In the two hours we waited, fifteen planes took off for the British Isles. Could mean a staggering number of deliveries over a period of time. We're all given warm, fleece, flying suits and boots. They tell us it's extremely cold over the North Atlantic. We take off at 6:15 P.M. and at 6:30 we're leaving the coast. At last over the ocean. Everybody takes off his parachute. I'm astounded. I ask why? A Royal Air Force officer tells me, "If we go down over the drink, old boy, it's not going to do you a bloody bit of good." They all laughed when I told them I felt better with it on, and that I hoped there would be no occasion for me to have the last laugh.

There's courage in everyone's eye. Mine, too, much to my surprise. Maybe in a tight little group like this, exposed to danger, everybody's courage gets all mixed up and you draw what you need from the common lot. The second pilot just assigned us our rubber life boats and "Mae Wests"—"just in case." We all laughed and jerked "thumbs up."

Into the night. I play games again. I'm Lindbergh crossing the Atlantic in *The Spirit of St. Louis*. Looking out of my small window at the shining heavenly bodies in the moonlit vastness, I feel a point-in-space loneliness that he and all the first ocean flyers must have known—a sense of danger, diluted by an exalting awareness of the infinite. It's hard to sustain a mystical experience with the plane rattling as if it's coming apart and the roar of four propeller engines in your ears. And these bucket seats aren't designed for comfort. Maybe if I stretch out on the floor I can catch some sleep. My thick flying suit and parachute should soften it a little. . . . I tried and failed. Even heavier vibration there.

We're flying against the night, and like two trains passing we're suddenly in the clear of another day.

A few more hours and the rocky isles of southern Ireland miraculously appear. Flight engineer calls out, "Another hour and a half till we put down in Scotland." I'm Lindbergh again, joyously sighting land!

Even flying at 10,000 feet over Ireland you understand why an Irishman can't speak of his county without rhapsodizing. Never have I seen such a lush green panorama.

Had a sudden sick feeling that we were fast descending to an emergency landing on a farm. Not until we touched down did I realize it was Presswick Airport in Scotland. Amazingly camouflaged! Terraced to look like the surrounding farm acres. Buildings and hangers all nestled under the foliage of clusters of trees or in haystacks. Planes landing and taking off every few minutes. The smell of war is getting stronger. As we climbed out of the belly of our Liberator, a small electric baggage truck, manned—rather womanned—by three overall-clad, grimy-faced young girls, drove up. They started slinging the heavy suitcases around like longshoremen. My first contact with the British people at war.

The flight took only twenty-three hours!

Went into the airport restaurant and blithely ordered ham and eggs. The waitress laughed. She thought my casualness part of my little joke. It suddenly hit me. Food is severely rationed here. I laughed with the waitress, pretending I had intended the joke. But when she asked if I'd take tea or coffee and I said tea, and from force of habit added, "with lemon, please," she really got sore. "Look 'ere mister," she said, "we ain't seen a lemon for three years. So don't go gettin' funny about it!"

The half crowns, shillings, pennies and ha'pennies I had been given confused me, and while trying to figure which coins would cover my check, I apologized to the cashier for holding up the line. I told her, "I'm sorry, I'm not used to English money." She sizzled and sharply replied, "In Scotland, sir-r-r, we dunnae call it English money, we say Br-r-r-ritish money!"

A special little two-seater had been sent up to fly me down to London. I was more frightened on that short trip than during the ocean crossing. The pilot seemed to be playing his own game of how close can he come to the tree tops. I think he missed one by a sixteenth of an inch.

July 26: Arrived London. Exhausted. Called Corwin to reassure him I'd be at rehearsal tomorrow. He was enormously relieved. Driven to Savoy Hotel. Strange—creeping along without headlights through totally blacked-out city. Flopped in bed. Slept for fifteen hours solid.

Monday, July 27: Learned I had slept through two alerts. Took cab to BBC Studios. Saw many ruins on the way. Everything still has an air of unreality. Maybe because I came so quickly from untouched America. I feel as if I'm the only real character moving through some monumental fiction.

Broadcast House—my destination. A little, round building at the end of Regent Street. This couldn't be the headquarters of the renowned BBC? Looked more like a pill box on the Maginot line. Ah, but wait. Enter and you go down, down, down till you come to the studios, large and small, snugly secure as an air-raid shelter, safe from all but a direct hit.

Happily greeted by Corwin and Ed Murrow, chief of CBS European Bureau, who is acting as producer of the series.

This is the first such expedition in radio history—a live dramatic series originating abroad, to promote good will between two countries by sending back the story of how the common people of Britain are bearing up under three years of war. The program is costly and risky, and CBS is showing great courage in undertaking it.

A lot of controlled excitement in the air. Corwin spent a lot of time on the phone with New York, testing sound effects. Since this is a pioneering project, there is no other way of knowing how certain effects will survive the shortwave crackle.

I was given my script to study. I am to play Norman Corwin, who is the *real* "American in England"—the program being about his first impressions of England at war.

The sixty-two piece Royal Air Force Orchestra was rehearsing an original score, composed by a sensitive, curly-haired smiling young man stalking about the studio, named Benjamin Britten. A CBS secretary told me she had trouble mailing him his fee. It was returned because he'd been forced out of his furnished room for not being able to pay his rent. [Just recalled I borrowed a book from him—thirty-two years ago! Must remember to return it sometime.]

While we were putting the show together, there was an air raid. A long alert. Around midnight, still no all-clear. The show was to go on at 4 A.M., so it could be heard at 10 P.M. in New York. We were given orders to move the entire production to a

BBC emergency studio. More than a hundred of us were involved—musicians, actors, technicians. [Some contrast with the
one- or two-man talk shows typical of today's radio program-
ing.] We all piled into cars and cabs, and somehow made our
way through the blackout to the barnlike BBC studios at
Maida Vale on the outskirts of London. These were the latest
emergency studios, improvised after a couple of others had
been bombed out.

Rehearsals honed the show to a sharp edge of readiness as
4 A.M. approached.

The opening words of the show were: "Hello? . . . Hello?
What's the matter with this line?" I, the American of the title,
presumably in New York making a reservation for my flight to
London, was having difficulty with the phone connection. Corwin deliberately used this as an ear-catching device, on the
theory that nothing rivets an audience's attention like something gone wrong. Great tension. Most of America listening—
everyone in the radio world. Friends tuned in—to find out if I
had landed safely.

Finally went on the air. Everything clicked. Everybody happy.
Mutual congratulations. A studio full of exhausted satisfaction.

A good night's sleep. Phoned Corwin to find out if there were
reports from America. There were, indeed! He and Ed Murrow
had taken a little walk after the broadcast. Murrow had not
wanted to tell him in front of the British, but he had learned
that when the CBS engineers in New York heard me say the
opening words, "Hello? . . . Hello? . . . What's the matter
with this line?" they thought the simulated disconnection was
real—that something had actually gone wrong. So, they pulled
their plugs, and put on a stand-by orchestra. America never
heard that broadcast. The ear-catching device was too real. We
were dismayed. But it gave Corwin an extra week to write the
second script, and me some time to explore this bustling embattled city.

July 29: Beautiful moonlit night. Long walk in the deserted streets. Moonglow on roofs of blacked-out buildings give them an eerie quality. London is like a gigantic ghost town—an abandoned city. Five minutes after return to hotel, gunfire! My first. Going downstairs!

Sirens sounded. An alert. Firing was the "ack-ack." There were many people in the lobby, in their pajamas and robes, waiting for the all-clear. As I returned to my room some of the flaming flack from the anti-aircraft shells was floating past my window. For the first time, I have a personal sense of danger here.

My phone just rang. A polite, male voice: "Would you mind drawing your curtains properly, please?" About a three-inch sliver of light was showing.

Heard explosions I was sure were bombs. The hotel shook. My heart was pounding. Learned they were ordinary anti-aircraft guns, but located close by. There had been a long lull in the saturation bombing that had devastated so much of the city, and people were fearful something new was about to happen.

July 30: 2 A.M.: Sat on the stone steps of Trafalgar Square, arms around my knees, looking up. Another moonlit night that cancels the blackout. Barrage balloons hanging in the sky. Can't understand their function. Do they carry nets to snare enemy planes? Seems to me bombers needn't come that low, and if they do they're spaced far enough apart to go through easily. I asked a young Canadian soldier what he thought they were good for. "Why, don't you know?" he said. "They hold the island up." Siren screamed an alert. Huge flashes in the sky synchronize with the boom of anti-aircraft guns. A young Tommy explains that a few Nazi planes come over every night about this time. They've dropped their bombs on the Midland factories, and on their way home, fly over London, just to start the alerts, wake the people up—keep them from getting their proper sleep. Which, I suppose, can be translated into a military value.

Corwin asked me to do a little research for him by accompanying a typical English working-class woman on her daily marketing. Mrs. Bave, a cleaning woman, took some pride in the fact that her neighborhood was mostly made up of cleaning women. "A lot of them even clean at the Ministry," she boasted. Her boy had left to be inducted that morning. When I asked her how she felt about it, she said, "I believe in patriotism and all that, but when 'e's your own boy . . . I believe in patriotism, but—" I noticed a plot of about twenty small vegetable gardens in the courtyard of her apartment house. I asked Mrs. Bave if she raised some of her own vegetables there. "We started to," she said, "but my 'usband, 'e wants to plant seeds one day and see them up the next. Besides, 'e's so busy at the factory 'e doesn't 'ave the time. So we gave our allotment to someone who would make better use of it."

We walked a few "turnings" to the grocers—like an average neighborhood grocery in America—except you feel they don't sell things, they apportion them. Much time is taken up discussing how many ration coupons should be cut from which book, etc. Each customer usually shops for several people, and so carries several ration books. A wrinkled old woman, with a shawl over her head, held up her own dirty paper bag for her allowance of two eggs. She had brought it to save the grocer's paper. The grocer addressed them all, "We only got fifty-three eggs this week—some bad ones." Everyone reacted to this. Much worried chatter. "I hope that includes my five"; "I didn't get my three last week"; etc.

GROCER: Boy gone, Mrs. Bave?

MRS. BAVE: Yes.

GROCER: Expect 'e'll be 'appier, 'e will.

MRS. BAVE: Yes.

August 12: Been here over two weeks now. Beginning to penetrate the shell of strangeness and see the English character, traditionally at its best in adversity. Their stiff upper lipism is frequently mocked, but there is something so real and rocklike at its core that nine months of daily blitz couldn't shatter it, and you can't imagine anything that would. The first attacks sent them reeling, but they recovered their national manners and counterattacked with a barrage of courage, wit, and contempt that wrecked Hitler's plan for systematically softening them up. He could have softened them more by leaving them alone. I have heard many stories of their behavior during air raids that could only be told of Englishmen. For example: A man in charge of a Civil Defense Depot told me how, in the middle of a bad one, he was at his desk answering requests for ambulances on the phone, when a thousand-pound bomb exploded nearby. It blew in the walls of his office and his desk collapsed on his lap. He and his young secretary were stunned—then looked at each other. She broke the silence. "Would you like a cup of tea, sir?" she asked. And she wasn't trying to be funny. She climbed over the rubble and in a few minutes returned with a pot of hot tea. He hadn't the slightest idea where she got it.

A popular expression when a bomb explodes close by is: "Quiet, beast!" out of the corner of the mouth. Women make dresses from the silk of parachutes the Nazis use to float down land mines (so they don't dig deep holes in the ground before exploding)—a good symbol of how Hitler's plans keep backfiring. The English even make the ruins fight back. They turn some of them into water reservoirs for fire fighters, using the rubble to construct them. They're marked by signs: "Sumps for Pumps."

An Englishman in the Savoy lobby told me: "I wish I had some way of telling America this, because one day they're going to get it, sure as hell. They don't know a damn thing about blast. They think it's just the explosion that does the damage. Blast! I've seen things you couldn't believe caused by blast. I was out in one of the raids and I heard a terrific screaming in what was left of one apartment building. Right in the middle of a room half-blown away was a girl in her late twenties—stark naked except for one stocking and one shoe—screaming her lungs out. 'What's the matter with you?' I said. 'Isn't it terrible?' she said, and screamed again. 'Stop it now, stop it,' I said. It was getting on my nerves, that screaming, more than the bombing, and I slapped her twice across the face. 'You ought to be ashamed of yourself sitting around naked in a raid,' I said. She started crying. 'I wasn't naked,' she said, and took me into her bedroom. 'Look!' She pointed to what was left of the walls. The force of the blast had pulled off all her clothes, including a heavy coat, and projected every piece of them into the plaster of the walls and ceiling. I can tell you plenty of stories about blast. You're going to lose a lot of people in New York before you learn about blast. Little things about not only lying down, but keeping off your stomach by folding your hands underneath you. And keeping your mouth open—and putting a handkerchief or a piece of rubber between your teeth or you'll have them smashed. Many things. Blast is mysterious and dangerous."

An American flying instructor, as we went out to watch the sky during an alert: "One thing the Germans have on the British. They use their searchlights effectively. You fly over the Ruhr industrial area and it's like daylight. They have a hell of a concentration of lights, and you just can't get out of it. We've lost a lot over there. But here over London, or anywhere here—they shoot a couple of beams at 'em, but it don't do a damn bit of good."

A blimpish Englishman overheard in the Savoy Bar: ". . . so I said to this American, 'Tell me, frankly, what is your impression of English women?' And he said, 'In America we bury our dead.'" His friend: "That reminds me of the story about the American soldier who was arrested here after a raid for raping a dead woman in a bombed-out building. The judge asked him why he committed such a disgusting crime. 'Plenty of girls around Piccadilly Circus, if that's the sort of thing you want, why must you rape a dead woman in a bombed-out building?' 'Dead?' the soldier exclaimed, 'I thought she was just English!'" They both laughed as only upper-class Englishmen can, and the first one said, "And they say we English cawn't tell jokes on ourselves!"

I auditioned English actors for Corwin. Quite a number were used in the series. My debut as a casting director. No job for me. I empathize too much. Felt terrible when I had to reject an actor. Especially well-known ones whom I had seen do fine work in films, but who couldn't adjust to microphone technique.

After the first week's mishap, the shows all went well. Reports from America were enthusiastic. *Variety* and other media reviews were raves. Here is Landry's comment in *Variety*, dated August 5, 1942:

An American in England
With Joseph Julian
30 Minutes.
Monday, 10 P.M.
WABC-CBS, New York

Norman Corwin's series after a complete failure the week before had a practically complete success Monday night (3) when the reception was remarkably satisfactory. Moreover, he actually succeeded at one point in deliberately burlesquing short-wave on shortwave transmission, mingling sound effects and assorted blended tidbits of English music and getting the whole thing through to American radio listeners. . . .

While some might consider fewer "yeas" and "huhs" necessary to round out the typical American, on the whole Corwin took his imaginary Yank across the Atlantic on a clipper and through to London in a style that was poignant, believable, and rich in clear mental pictures. It should add up to a net contribution to British-American understanding.

Himself a first visitor to England it is likely that Corwin has come remarkably close to epitomizing the mixed sentiments and impressions of the average American who finds the tight little island a bit strange but likeable. The script was dotted with interesting sidelights, just the sort of detail tourists always are interested in and struck by. The kind of food you can't get, the kind of delays you face, the patience needed to contract for a taxicab, compared to which Washington cab service is a model of alacrity. By adding up the details, wholly without melodrama, a panorama of war came through. The waste and heartache and the bravery and horror became clearer.

Musically the program had a 50 piece RAF symphony orchestra. That was unnecessary as a small unit would have sufficed and shortwave transmission is not the ideal medium for big orchestras. Joseph Julian, who followed Corwin to England to enact the narrator role, proved an excellent choice, his versatile reading being from both the brain and heart. Contrived wholly in the first person present tense, the script was masterful in achieving an even, unjerky unfoldment. Various English voices were brought in and out, some just for action and color, one or two to talk about the war. The soliloquizing was especially adroit in allowing the tourist to first mention and then have enacted the typical American misconceptions of English character, the silly ass lord, the variety hall cockney singer. Amusing, too, was Corwin's use of the quaint conceit which appeals to Americans, namely that the BBC would remain impeccably itself if announcing one evening on the 11 P.M. newscast that the world had come to an end but the Government was, for the moment, withholding comment.

Corwin continues to discharge difficult tasks of rare tact, feeling and imagination with great artistry.

John K. Hutchens, writing in the New York Sunday *Times* on August 16, 1942:

. . . *An American in England* finds Mr. Corwin once more writing with a poet's vision, a good reporter's clarity and a technician's precise knowledge of his craft—three attributes that have made him preeminent in radio literature. Now he is part story-teller, part travel writer, looking at a friendly, foreign land with inquiring gaze and understanding heart, speaking through a narrator who is presumably any young American visiting England for the first time and bringing with him certain preconceived notions but a willingness to learn. The narrator, Joseph Julian, tells the tale in prose, but frequently the effect is of poetry; for even when he is in a more or less realistic vein, Mr. Corwin writes in phrases that lift the heart . . . Everything is done in little touches, but the cumulative effect is profoundly stirring. . . . Mr. Corwin honors the good, average, unspectacular people by writing of them quietly, warmly, personally, with the intimacy and detail of a good travel letter that catches not only the moment but the vast implications behind it. This is a distinguished program by an artist, major work in a minor key.

Each weekly show had a different title and theme. "London by Clipper" described Corwin's flight over and his first impressions of embattled London. "London to Dover" was the second of the series, and dealt with his various small encounters with the people of those communities. "Women at War" was about just that. It conveyed how much of Britain's resistance was due to her effective use of woman power in factories and wherever a job was left open by a man who had joined the Armed Forces. Other titles were "The Anglo-American Angle," which stressed our common interests, and "Cromer"—which is the name of a town. The first page of the Cromer script looked like this:

STUDIO ANNOUNCER: Cromer is a town on the east coast of England, and this is a program about it. The program has to do with bombs and a postmaster and a rescue squad and an old church and a Spitfire and several other matters, and it takes a half hour.

MUSIC: Quiet introductory theme, sustaining behind:

NARRATOR: A town is like a person. It has a character, a com-
plexion, and a name. It has a set of habits. It's hardworking or
lazy, rich or poor, handsome or ugly. Some towns never
amount to much; some get sick and die; some grow big and
powerful and lead their race.

But all towns, be they so great they call themselves metropo-
lises or so small you'd miss them if you winked while driving
through—all towns have this in common; they are mortal. They
know seasons and the way of winds, each taking its share of
sun and moon and standing up to storm. And they are mortal
also in the respect of violence and death. For war may come to
any and to all of them.

Troy was a town.

So was Jericho.

Lidice was a town.

Likewise Our Lady the Queen of the Angels of Porciuncula,
later to be known as Los Angeles.

And Cromer was a town and is a town, and you'll find it on a
map of the east coast of England, in the ancient division of the
country called East Anglia, facing the North Sea—facing Germany.

And then listeners were introduced to the residents of
Cromer, Corwin's thoughts about them, and their thoughts
about themselves.

The *American in England* series, although highly
praised, did not break any rating records in the United
States. It was aired opposite Bob Hope. What was more,
he didn't have to buck transatlantic static.

The British radio people were enormously impressed
with Corwin, not only for his warm appreciation of their
country's war effort, but because his sharp, clean writing
and production techniques were a revelation to "Old
Aunty," as the government-run, somewhat stodgy BBC
was sometimes referred to by Britons.

But there was nothing stodgy about its wartime function of alleviating the despair of millions, secretly huddled around clandestine receiving sets in the Axis-subjugated countries of Europe. Around the clock, and in dozens of languages, it poured out messages of hope and news that could be relied upon. The BBC became a shining monument of truth, to allies and enemies alike.

Val Gielgud, the brother of Sir John, and the then head of the BBC Dramatic division, invited me to star in a radio version of the American play, *They Knew What They Wanted*, by Sidney Howard. I had plenty of time for it since Corwin's shows were a week apart, and I was only needed for two days of rehearsal. My co-star was the lovely Constance Cummings, a fine American actress who had married the British playwright Ben Levy. It was a gratifying engagement—for a reason I shall explain later.

It has been said that an actor is a sculptor in snow. Throughout the six weeks of the *An American in England* series, I tried to think of myself as a sculptor in better relations between Britain and America. Each Monday at 4 A.M., as I approached the microphone in the bombproof, subterranean studio of the BBC, I had no thought of playing a part, of getting inside a character, of doing an acting job. Just before the "on the air" sign lit up, I'd have a quick little talk with myself that went something like this:

> Well, Julian, about 10,000,000 Americans are listening, go ahead now, talk to them. Tell them what you've seen with your own eyes. Tell your country what it's like under the Nazi guns. Help them understand the British people and the urgency of the war. Tell them what it's like—but borrow Corwin's words to do it.

Came the downbeat for the sixty-two musicians—a cue to me—and I "borrowed" Corwin's words.

Identifying with his words came easily. Although he dramatized his experiences and observations, we were both "Americans in England." For the most part, we went to the same places, and saw similar things to which we reacted in pretty much the same way. His scripts were largely documentation of my own impressions. I have never had an acting job where the author's frame of reference so closely coincided with my own. In fact, one of my own experiences almost wound up as a scene in one of the shows.

Strolling around blacked-out Piccadilly Circus one evening, I struck up a conversation with a young black American GI, and what he told me so touched and pained me that when I left him I hurried back to the hotel and wrote down our dialogue, almost verbatim:

J.J.: You American?
GI: Yeah.
J.J.: So am I. Where you from?
GI: Pittsburgh. Where you from?
J.J.: New York.
GI: I worked there at the Savoy in Harlem for a while.
J.J.: I was up there just before I left.
GI: (brightening) Yeah? Whose band was playin'?
J.J.: I forget.
GI: They sent me first to Oklahoma an' then back to Fort Dix. I gotta gal out in Brooklyn I went to see one night. I was a sergeant an' they busted me for it.
J.J.: Why?
GI: AWOL. See, she had a kid from me an' I wanted to see both of 'em before I came over here. Didn't know if I'd ever come

back again so, I wanted to see 'em. I made out an allotment to her.

J.J.: That's tough, being busted for that.

GI: I don't blame 'em. Gotta have rules in an army. I'm a corporal now.

J.J.: How do you like it here?

GI.: All right—'cept not many colored boys over here. Ya get lonesome sometimes.

J.J.: How do the English treat you?

GI.: Oh, hell, they treat ya fine. It's in the camp and around we get all the trouble and riots.

J.J.: You mean with American soldiers?

GI: Yeah. We had three officers resign last week. They didn' want nuthin' ta do with us.

J.J.: White officers?

GI: Yeah. Lotta them white boys still look at us like we ain't nuthin'—just ta shine their shoes. They walk away from me when I walk down the street. They go out when I come into a pub for a drink. They change their seats when I sit down in a movie. . . . [At that precise moment, two drunken American sailors staggered up to us. One of them plopped his arm on the corporal's shoulder and said, "Hey, Darkie, we're broke. Could you let us have some change?" Without a second's hesitation the corporal reached in his pocket, took out a half crown, and dropped it in the white sailor's hand. There was a pause, then he continued]: I have a friend came over here in 1936 with a band an' married an English girl. I was talkin' to them one day. He went across the street to get a paper, I stayed talkin' to his wife. Three white American soldiers came by, seen me talkin' to a white girl, an' they ripped her furpiece off an' tore it to pieces.

J.J.: Do you go into any of the American Service clubs here? Red Cross, and so forth?

GI: I just keep by myself. I don' go lookin' for trouble no more. But sometimes when I drive a truck down from Birmingham where I'm stationed, I have to stay in London overnight, so I got to a British soldier club an' they put me up. At the American clubs when they do give you a bed they make ya feel they don' wanna.

J.J.: How do most Negro soldiers feel about the war?

GI: I think we feel it don' matter much what happens. We just know we have ta fight so we fight.

J.J.: But you feel much more comfortable in the company of English soldiers?

GI: Sure, man. They drink with ya, they talk with ya. There ain't no difference with them. I'd like to stay here after the war. 'Cept the United States is still your home, an' ya have a feelin' ya wanna get back to your home no matter how bad things are there.

J.J.: Well, I hope it will work out. That's one thing this war is supposed to be about. So long, soldier, I have to run along.

GI: Take it easy. An' if ya ever get up around Sheldon, Birmingham—that's where I'm stationed—stop in an' have some chow with us.

J.J.: Thanks, I will.

I phoned Corwin in his room, told him of the dialogue I had just recorded. I said that I believed it important enough to incorporate in his next script. He immediately came down to the Savoy lobby, read it, and agreed with me that it simply and eloquently expressed the feelings of the average Negro with the American Expeditionary Forces in England, and should be reported to the people back home; he said however that Ed Murrow would have to approve it.

I had, of course, known of Edward R. Murrow as a famous and courageous radio correspondent who had flown dangerous missions with the Air Force over Germany and was constantly putting his life on the line to bring CBS listeners accurate and vivid pictures of the landscape of war. Every evening, along with millions of other Americans, I had ritually tuned in and thrilled to his cryptic opening line, "This is London," followed by the news in measured words and aggressively mellow tones that plowed, undaunted, through the hostile shortwave atmospherics. It was not only his voice that hooked listeners. There was something special about this man, and people sensed it. I believe they basically responded to his great honesty and integrity. And his deceptively subdued manner concealed an enormous capacity for moral indignation—as I personally discovered on this, and a future occasion.

The next morning Corwin and I met in Murrow's office. I showed him my dialogue with the corporal. His eyes gleamed, he banged a fist in his palm, and said, "Let's do it! Let's raise a little hell back home!" I was greatly pleased at the prospect of contributing something extra to the series. As he poured us each a whiskey I had my first long look at this interesting man, with the inevitable cigarette dangling from his lips. I think my strongest impression was that of superbly controlled tension. In repose, his face had a brooding, Lincolnesque sadness that would quickly dissolve in the sudden flash of his warm smile.

Although Murrow was a man of action and a fighter for what he believed in, I sensed an undertow of pessimism dragging at his spirit. As chief of CBS's European Bureau, he lived war day and night. When I asked him what he did to unwind, he gave me a rather surprising answer. "I go back to the Greeks," he said. "Right now I'm rereading Socrates and Plato. I always find something there to hang on to."

It struck me as strange that in the midst of the carnage and despite his commitment to the defeat of the Nazis, Murrow felt the need to search out support for his own personal faith. He showed me a snapshot of his small son. "To take him fishing is more important than anything else," he said.

The next day he told us that he had had second thoughts about using my scene. He decided that this would be the wrong moment to "raise a little hell back home," that a unified home front was more urgent at this time than stressing a divisive issue. Deferentially, I disagreed, and advanced a rather abstract argument about the military value of truth. But it was his honest conviction, and he was firm. He suggested I work the material up into an article for publication. "But don't wait until you get home," he said, "or you probably won't. Write it now while you have your full load of anger." I followed his advice. (A few months after I returned it was published in *The Nation*, under the title, "Jim Crow Goes Abroad.") *

The incident stimulated an urge to write something of my own for radio, and I began to make more notes on my experiences, intending to make something of them—I didn't know quite what—when I got back.

While jotting in my notebook on the beach at Dover, I felt a sudden, heavy hand on my shoulder. I wheeled around and looked up into the face of a policeman, who politely demanded to know what the hell I was doing there, sketching the beach defenses. I showed him my papers and assured him I was with CBS radio and was

* December 5, 1942.

only writing my impression of Dover's famous white cliffs. "You better not do it around 'ere," he said. "You're libel to hear a loud suckin' noise and find yourself in the clink."

Dover was strictly off-limits to all but the armed forces and the native population, most of whom stubbornly refused to leave, and those with special permission. I had told Murrow of my desire to visit England's most famous front-line town, and he had arranged it with the Ministry.

This incredible little community on the English Channel was only twenty-one miles from the enemy. On a clear day, with field glasses, you could see farmers working the land in France. This proximity, and the fact that it was one of Britain's most important naval bases, meant that Dover saw more continuous military action than any other theater of World War II. Hardly a day passed without air raids, shelling, dog fights, ack-ack, convoy battles, motor torpedo boat attacks, or exploding mines. The waterfront bristled with barbed wire and anti-aircraft guns. The unhealthiest-looking seashore I ever saw.

The strongest impression of my day in Dover was of the quiet heroism of the residents.

The white chalk hills held, probably, the safest air-raid shelters in the world. A honeycomb of spacious, well-stocked tunnels, some more than three miles long, could accommodate the entire Dover population of 20,000. Those who were bombed out used them for homes, but most residents wouldn't go into them during alerts. After living for three years in a constant state of alert, they developed a kind of therapeutic fatalism. I asked a Dover butcher if it wasn't foolish having such splendid shelters and not using them. He answered: "Good Lord, man, do you know we have sometimes ten or twelve alerts in one day. Do you know what that would mean if we went to the shelters each time? We wouldn't get a bloody thing done. We must carry on our work under fire just as our soldiers do. They don't leave their gun positions when they're attacked."

I also talked to the postmaster of a demolished sub-station along the beach. An old man of eighty-one, he had gathered a few boards and built a little shed in the middle of the ruins where he continued his postal services. I asked why he didn't continue his work from the safer main post office up toward the center of town. He shook his head vigorously:

POSTMASTER: No sir! See those five or six houses up the beach?
J.J.: Yes.
POSTMASTER: That was a solid row once—of about fifteen.
J.J.: Bombs?
POSTMASTER: Those empty spaces were shell hits. Well sir, several old women live in those houses. They're between seventy-five and one hundred years old. One old gentleman is one hundred and two. They live on pensions. We've tried a hundred times to get them to move, but they just won't budge. Now, they're too old to walk up the hill to the main office. Somebody's got to stay down here with a place they can come to every week to get their pension checks, and to give them their cup of hot chocolate.

When I asked some Doverites why they hadn't evacuated when the government asked them to, some answers were:

MAN: I've been dive-bombed, high-bombed, machine-gunned, and our house was brought down around us by a shell, but we're sticking it until we win, and then my wife and I are going on a jolly good holiday.

WOMAN: This shelling isn't nice but we can stick it.
OLD WOMAN: I like this town. I won't move away for no one. And I want to tell Mr. Hitler that if he steps on the bulldog's tail—it'll bite him.

Many Americans mistake British imperturbability for coldness. They say they're without real emotions. I confess to having been a bit shocked at first by what seemed their almost morbid custom of understatement. For instance, this snatch of conversation I had with a young Tommy:

TOMMY: My aunt had a very nasty experience the other night.
J.J.: What happened?
TOMMY: Jerry was over and dropped one on her house.
J.J. A direct hit?
TOMMY: Yes.
J.J.: Was she badly hurt?
TOMMY: Blown to bits.

Almost like a grotesque vaudeville sketch. As was the seeming indifference of the Dover Air Raid Warden as he told me: "Yes, I was standin' 'ere talkin' to Joe, an' came a crump and a smack an' old Joe's head was blown clean off an' landed right at my feet."

Speaking of vaudeville, my doubts about the British were resolved when I went in to see a show at the Hippodrome, Dover's gallant little front-line theater that had carried on since the war began, come hell, Hitler, or high water.

As I entered, a strip-tease artist was doing her stuff. She had removed all her clothes and was coyly holding a loose black cloth in front of her, as she sang in a squeaky voice and with exaggerated naïveté:

Only a rose in my hair—
No pretty gown to see.
But you don't seem to care.
What *do* you see in me?

But I was fascinated more by the audience. Not a hoot, not
a whistle, not a "Take it off!"—not a sound out of that
packed house of English Tommies and Tars. It was like a
church. At that point I was almost convinced English
blood *is* diluted with ice water. Then, teasingly, the lady
stepped down three steps into the audience. Slowly, deliberately, she took the rose from her hair and held it out to a
soldier in the front row. Closer and closer she came—
silence. Then a wee small voice in the back said, "Grab
it!" The entire front row of men jumped from their seats
and lunged at her, but, being an artist, she stepped nimbly
aside and ran back to the safety of the stage. The legendary English "reserve" had finally succumbed to the impetus of that one tiny voice. My faith in the English was
renewed.

I stayed overnight in a tavern on the edge of a cliff over-
looking the English Channel, run by a Mrs. Moore and her
twelve-year-old daughter, June. The Battle of Britain had
mainly been fought in the air directly above them. Mrs.
Moore described some of what they lived through.

"British pilots over the Continent, trying so desperately
to get back home, would so strain their engines that they'd
overheat and explode and fall all around our place. Many
who just pancaked in crashed and died."

She told me that the Nazis never bombed the tavern
because it was a good landmark for their raiders. Little
June became such an expert on the different types of aircraft that the Ministry of Defense would frequently tele-

phone her and ask her to identify Nazi planes that crossed the Channel. She knew every plane the enemy had and could even tell them apart from the sound of their motors.

That evening I stood outside with June, on the highest point of the highest cliff, and for the first time saw Nazi guns in action as the quick, sharp flashes of their anti-aircraft fire stabbed the black night on the French side of the Channel. June was talking plane talk, trying to make me understand the meaning of wing measurement in relation to bomb load and how the displacement of the fuselage in certain kinds of craft was important in relation to . . . Suddenly she interrupted herself, looked at her watch, and let out a little cry.

"Oh, you must excuse me," she said. "I do have to run. I'm late for the cinema. Errol Flynn is playing tonight in *Captain Blood!*" And she ran off to the real excitement in her life.

I left England on September 14, 1942, steeped in impressions, and with the deep conviction that under that British reserve were other great reserves, of physical and psychic strength, which would see these people through to victory.

Flying home in a Pan American Clipper ship (the first transatlantic passenger service) was much more comfortable than the way I had come, cramped in the crude belly of a Liberator bomber. Most people don't know how luxurious those early flying boats were. Taking off and landing on water, they had many of the accommodations of today's flying hotels—double-decked, a cocktail lounge, and full-length beds that folded out if one wished to sleep. The flight took twenty-seven hours and was most pleasant—except for one constant irritant—the man in the seat next to me. Gray-haired, around fifty, he loved to talk. Especially did he love to tell jokes, and his supply was inexhaustible. He was a compulsive entertainer, totally insensitive to my hollow responses. My head was swirling with images of what I had seen and done in London, but he went on and on, even when I closed my eyes and pretended to fall asleep. There were moments when I wanted to scream, "Goddammit, please, sir! Let me alone with my private thoughts!" But I just couldn't bring myself to say that to the man. After all, it was Al Jolson.

A soft bump and a long swish: we had landed in Flushing Bay, at LaGuardia Airport. Back to beautiful, unbombed New York. Reporters and photographers clustered around, and flashbulbs popped as we disembarked. Not only for Al Jolson, who had been entertaining American troops all over the British Isles; everyone on that plane was newsworthy, for flying the ocean in those days gave one automatic celebrity status. In fact, so few had done it that those who had were considered members of an elite, unorganized organization called The Short Snorters. The membership card was a dollar bill signed by one's fellow passengers. Why the title? When two members met anywhere in the world, at either's request, they were supposed to have a short snort (a quick drink) together. For a long time afterward I kept hoping I would run into the peripatetic Eleanor Roosevelt, so I could flash my dollar bill at her.

The day after my return, William Paley, president of CBS, invited me to his office to give him my personal impression of things in war-torn London. The latent reporter in me urged him to send me to Africa and other fronts with the newly invented portable "wire" recorder to record interviews with American soldiers. He promised to think about it.

The success of the *American in England* series, and the attendant publicity, greatly increased my prestige. It brought an invitation to read a poem at Carnegie Hall about artists who had died fighting Fascism (which was to get me in great trouble years later) and it also brought me a lot of work, which I sorely needed. For thanks to my great head for business, my London adventure had actually ended up costing me money.

In those days—1942 and 1943—the airwaves were saturated with dramas, and I began getting calls for most of them. Soon I was averaging twenty to twenty-five shows a month. To give you an idea of their variety, here's a list from my records of a typical month in 1943:

> *Joyce Jordon, Girl Interne*
> *Inner Sanctum*
> *Grantland Rice Sport Stories*
> *Mr. District Attorney*
> *Out of the Shadows*
> *Broadway Matinee*
> *Bulldog Drummond*
> *Community Chest* drama
> *Labor for Victory*
> *The Thin Man*
> *Famous Jury Trials*
> *Superman*
> *Reader's Digest*
> *Front Page Farrell*
> *True Story*
> *Chaplain Jim*
> *Gangbusters*

Counterspy
Believe It or Not
New World a Comin'
Words at War
Men of the Sea
Stella Dallas
This Changing World
Charlie Chan
The Goldbergs
The Deerslayer
The March of Time

There were also a number of programs on the air that purported to be non-fiction: *My True Story, True Life Stories, Aunt Jenny's Real Life Stories,* etc. They weren't. But they dealt with basic emotions and happy endings, and so were among the most popular shows on the air.

The *Radio Reader's Digest,* a prime-time evening hour, was an exception. Each week it did relatively authentic dramatizations of real-life stories from the *Reader's Digest.* One evening, however, there was a side plot no one bargained for. The scene was a hospital operating room. To feature the effect of the patient's heart beating, the director had the sound effects man press a stethoscope against the actor's heart, while holding the listening end very close to the microphone. The "thump, thump, thump" was most effective when integrated into the dialogue and story.

As the show signed off the air, the telephones at NBC began to ring. There were twenty-one calls, from twenty-one doctors, all over the United States, all urging the actor whose heartbeat was broadcast to rush immediately to a hospital. All twenty-one doctors had detected a malfunctioning heart. The actor heeded their advice. An electrocardiogram confirmed his condition; quite possibly his life had been saved by the twenty-one alert professionals. He was lucky they were tuned in. But then, with an audience of millions, there's always bound to be a doctor in the house.

One day in 1943, as I was leaving a CBS studio at 485 Madison Avenue after doing a show, who should be waiting for me in the lobby but Tom Ashwell.

What had happened to the big job at WXYZ in Detroit? He explained that his creditors from the West Coast had finally caught up with him, and their continual harassment had made it impossible for him to continue. But he had big plans and a number of offers in New York, including one to develop and produce a soap opera. For the moment, however, he was slightly strapped, and could I let him have ten dollars?

He asked for it without seeming to beg or demean himself, oblivious to the wrenching he had given my life eight years before. Within five minutes he had practically convinced me that losing his job as program manager of WXYZ had been another fast step up the ladder of success. Well, he had once said he would make it by being different. I gave him the ten bucks and wished him well.

After his return from England late in 1942, Norman Corwin had continued to concern himself almost exclusively with the war, and he continued to cast me in most of his shows. One, *El Capitan and the Corporal,* I fondly remember because of a special effect achieved during rehearsal. I played a soldier who falls in love with a girl on the train carrying him to war. The romance became urgent because he didn't know when, if ever, he would return. Katherine Locke (who later became Mrs. Corwin) played the girl. There was one scene that depended largely on sound effects—when the train had a short stop at a station and the soldier and the girl got out and somehow drifted away from the right track. There was much frantic running up and down stairs to different platform levels, calling out each other's name, as the train was about to leave. Two sound men—one with high heels—running in place on a concrete slab—didn't paint the precise sound picture Corwin wanted. We were in the basement studio of the CBS annex on 53rd Street, and just outside the door were stairs leading to the upper floors. Corwin decided to make them work for us. He placed low microphones on the steps, and others on several floor landings. This is how the scene played: I was narrating the story at a standing microphone in the studio. When I came to this scene I was given a hand mike by a little man, who (as I continued to read) guided me by the elbow out the studio door to the foot of the stairs. There, I gave him back the hand mike, which left me free to run up the stairs, calling out to Katherine who was on an upper level. She called out to me as she ran down the stairs. We both ran up and down several times, adlibbing, "Where are you?" "Here I am!" "Where's the train?" etc. The strategically placed mikes picked up our voices and authentic footsteps in proper perspective and made the action vividly clear to listeners. As the story returned to narration, I was again given the small hand mike, and as I spoke, reading from the script, was carefully led back into the studio, where I switched over again to the standing microphone. A lot of trouble for an effect that only lasted a few minutes? No question; but that's one of the reasons Corwin had no peer in radio.

He also had few in the fine low art of punning. A man of words, he loved to play with them, and occasionally got off a really good one. Once, during a rehearsal, I asked to be excused to go to the men's room. "Of course," Corwin said. "I always insist that my actors mind their pees and cues."

A double-barreled masterpiece.

Although I was kept busy on a great variety of dramas, a restlessness set in. The strong meat of my adventures in England made *Nick Carter, Master Detective* seem mightily irrelevant. The problems of *Our Gal Sunday* (Can a coal miner's daughter find happiness married to England's richest lord?) reminded me of the real problems of the London population facing instant extinction from the devastating buzz-bomb attacks Hitler had just launched. My memories of the heroic people of Dover wouldn't quiet down, and the notes I made of my day there kept bothering me to organize them into some kind of statement. Finally I did. I wrote and narrated a half hour documentary called *Dover Diary*. The American Broadcasting Company produced it over their Blue Radio Network on July 10, 1943.

Radio was an especially congenial medium for documentaries. Its flexibility allowed for rapid transitions and quick statements. Time could be telescoped by a montage of sounds; cold statistics conveyed by an actor projecting his voice dispassionately with equal emphasis on all syllables. Figures could be "billboarded" or underlined by putting an exclamation mark in the voice—the vocal equivalent of printing.

A great many documentaries were produced during radio's vigorous years, mostly by the networks, in non-commercial hours, set aside under federal law for public-service programming. During the war years, the Office of War Information (OWI) also produced a great many which were beamed abroad as propaganda.

7. If Memory Serves...

S ince I was now earning my living entirely from radio, I decided I owed it my best efforts. Instead of complaining about how it spoiled good actors I tried to bring to it an additional dimension.

From time to time I had experimented with learning my lines, wherever possible within radio's short rehearsal periods. During my stay in London I had been invited by the BBC to co-star with Constance Cummings in a two-hour radio version of Sidney Howard's play, *They Knew What They Wanted.* I was delighted to discover in Miss Cummings a kindred spirit who also had an aversion to acting from a script. With the understanding and encouragement of Val Gielgud, our director, we both memorized our roles. We related to each other as on a movie set or a stage. We moved about the studio with complete freedom to accommodate our impulses. When an exit was called for, we walked away. When we were supposed to touch, we touched. And the sound of a lover's kiss was not produced by a sound effects man sucking on the back of his hand. The engineers set up an overhead boom microphone that followed us around, instead of a stationary one like those in general use.

It was a most interesting experiment, and seemed to confirm my theory that if an actor were freed from his script and could better contact fellow actors on a visual as well as an oral level, it would stimulate truer emotion, enrich his performance, and give him more release as an artist. It did for me.

I found it fairly easy to do if the roles were not too long; and, except for the leads, most weren't. They generally amounted to a paragraph or two. I discovered three or four hours of rehearsal were enough for almost any actor to stuff that many lines in his head—if he applied himself. And so I began to memorize regularly as a working method. For short rehearsal periods, I developed a compromise technique of learning as much as I could, and marking places in the script where I was unsure, so my eye could quickly find it.

I was considered a bit of a nut by my peers. Why go to all that trouble when it really wasn't required; when it was so simple to read from the script? And the time between cues could be spent knitting or reading the paper—if you turned the pages quietly enough not to be picked up by the mike. But these were my fervent years, and I was determined to make my contribution to art and progress. I wrote another article setting forth my views. It was published in the Sunday *New York Times* on August 20, 1944:

A PLEA FOR BETTER RADIO ACTING
By Joseph Julian

Why is a radio actor? You almost never hear "He is a theater actor." True, they say "He is a movie actor," but they mean

"He works in the movies." But when they say "He is a radio actor" they don't always mean he works in radio. There is frequently an insinuated note of opprobrium in the term. Radio actors are not taken seriously as artists. This, I believe, is largely due to the fact that radio actors don't take themselves seriously as artists. Nor does the industry.

Radio writers have made tremendous strides. They're constantly experimenting with new techniques and have evolved many original, interesting ways of presenting their ideas. Directors, too, have pushed back their horizon and made room for a greater play of imagination. But radio acting seems to just keep meretriciously and phlegmatically rolling along.

Although radio offers more creative scope to the writer and director than to the actor, who is more inhibited by its mechanics, there is plenty of room for improvement between the present general level of radio acting and the limitations inherent in the medium itself. But this improvement will be effected only when actors, directors, and engineers cooperatively toss out some of their fixed notions of studio production.

Directors and engineers must develop a larger understanding of an actor's approach to his work. They should try harder to understand the creative acting process—not only the objective results. And they should do everything technically possible to facilitate this process by helping the actor create, in the studio, the greatest possible reality for himself of the scene he is playing.

THE SETTING

For example, I have discovered most actors deeply hunger for "contact" with their fellow performers at a microphone. Very often an engineer or director, in order to get a better voice balance, will have them play, let's say, an intimate love scene on separate mikes six feet apart. Even though it might achieve a better physical voice balance, the inner emotional balance of the performers suffers, and the inner honesty of a scene is more important.

Although not practical in every dramatic show, especially

those with many quick changes of scene, they could in most cases prepare for the actor at least an indication of a *mise en scène*. If the setting is the family dinner table, a mike should be put on a table with the actors sitting around it. If it's a hospital bed, let the actor lie down and bring a mike to him. Let him use actual hand properties whenever possible, etc. A few directors work this way, but unfortunately to most it's superfluous nonsense and a waste of time. Actors, however, and listeners, know the difference.

Now, what can the actors themselves do to help their profession grow up?

There are two fundamental ways any artist can look at his profession. He can either try to raise its standards by constantly striving to improve his own work, or he can merely aim at supplying a market. Radio has mostly market suppliers. Of course there are actors on the stage, and screen, too, to whom acting is primarily a business, but there is also a vanguard of serious-minded artists who work at their art. There are professionals in the theater who, even while working in Broadway shows, band together in their free time to discuss and study how better to use the tools of their craft.

WORDS VS. EMOTION

But as far as I know there is not and never has been a comparable group among radio actors. There are a few exceptions, but most radio actors, year after year, gallop from studio to studio, "leaning" on their scripts and shooting at nothing higher than a "good-enough-for-radio" performance. And while they develop a highly specialized facility for quick work, their performances are usually "indications" of something, rather than "something" itself.

Most roles in radio dramas are small ones. Generally they wouldn't add up to more than a few solid paragraphs. Surely these parts could be memorized in a few hours. Even actors with larger roles could work out a compromise technique of memorizing as much as possible. Memory is not as noncooperative as most of us believe. It only needs exercise to function well and with a little training can do amazing things.

UP FROM THE WISECRACK

Radio actors are people, too, and if they really identify themselves emotionally with the character they're playing they'll find their memories can do a pretty reliable job with the dialogue. I know a few actors who have experimented along these lines, and found themselves giving performances more satisfactory, both to themselves and to listeners, than they ever dreamed possible. There should be more experiments of this sort. Radio actors should free themselves from their bondage to scripts, and with the cooperation of directors and engineers learn to make their basic adjustment to the dramatic objectives of the story instead of to a microphone.

This, I believe, is the direction we must move in if our profession is to be rescued from its present status at the short end of a wisecrack.

There were letters to the editor on this one, too—mostly from actors—but nothing as explosive as from the *Variety* article of three years before. One actor vented his regard for my theories and talent in a long poem about his career in the theater and where do I get off to teach him anything.

> . . . I read in the paper on Sunday
> How most radio acting stinks,
> Written by a person
> Whose actin' is wors'n
> Even he or anyone thinks.
> Oh I've taken parts as I've found 'em.
> Just like Joe Julian;
> But the more that I see of the others
> The less I'll settle for him.
> It would help him to do some thinkin'

Before memorizing a radio show,
And be warned that a lot
Think he's not very hot
And won't learn about actin' from Joe.

As a proselytizer I think I was a total failure. I doubt if I made one real convert. Looking back, I can see that my crusading zeal blinded me somewhat to the disturbing effect my memorizing had on many actors with whom I worked. They resented it for several reasons. It implied a criticism of their work. It had a smart alec "Look ma no hands" aspect. And there was the matter of cues. I always made a point of trying to give exact cues. But memorizing per se has risks, and actors were frequently fearful of getting wrong or sloppy cues from me that would spoil their performance. I was aware of this and conscientiously tried always to give the cue that was in the script.

One evening, I failed. I was working *The Quentin Reynolds Show* on NBC, a program that dramatized the exploits of that renowned war correspondent. After rehearsing all afternoon, we had an hour's break before airtime, during which Reynolds invited me for a drink. (I had known him from the Savoy Bar in London, where we used to sit with RAF fighter pilots as they exchanged accounts of the day's dog fights, illustrating them with a graceful ballet of hands.) I had already learned the lines for my scene that evening, but because of the few drinks, I decided I had better not risk doing it from memory. So, when we later went on the air, I conscientiously read every single word from the script—and fluffed all over the place.

On another occasion my memorizing scared the hell out of Frederic March. It was a big Norman Corwin production over CBS entitled *Untitled* (yes, that's right), and I had a long, block speech as a soldier returned from war describing the horrors that had happened to his buddy. We rehearsed for a couple of days, which gave me time to fully learn the speech. I felt secure enough at airtime to go to the mike without the script in my hands. I usually held it at my side, or behind me to resort to in an emergency. This was the first time I dared "go it alone." March's mouth dropped open as I placed my script on my chair, and walked empty-handed to the microphone. I looked up to the glass control booth, where Corwin stood masterminding the elements of the show. A slow wave of his hand signaled the orchestra to segue to soft introductory music; a finger jabbed at the sound man started the footsteps; a nod of his head to me and I began.

It went well. Not only didn't I fluff, it was one of the really full moments I experienced in radio acting.

After the show, March told me how nervous I had made him. He had seized my script and with his finger traced each word as I spoke, ready to thrust it to me if I "went up." He remarked, as others frequently had, about my phenomenal memory. There was nothing phenomenal about it. I had had two full days to learn a one-page speech. In the early days of stock companies, actors learned full-length plays in less than a week.

However, I do have a theory about memory in relation to actors. I believe that if you serve it properly it will serve you. This applies to learning roles in all media. Actors can best learn lines by not trying too hard. The intention of the lines is more important. After reading through the script one or more times, the actor should first learn *why* the character he is playing says what he says. What is he trying to achieve? What is his intention, his action? Actions speak louder than words, and they're easier to memorize. And once he is clear about his action, the words, which have been quivering on the periphery of memory since the first reading of the script, are much more likely to jump into full consciousness voluntarily. Actors who have the most trouble memorizing are primarily those who learn the words first. These actors are lost if their memory suddenly fails. But the actor who is clear about his intention is always able to substitute another appropriate word or phrase to keep the scene alive and moving. If this smacks of Stanislavsky—so be it!

Almost a year and a half after its production, my *Dover Diary* brought me an offer to go to the other side of the world.

In December, 1944, Robert Saudek, Public Service director for the American Broadcasting Company, informed me that he had had an inquiry from an official of the Red Cross, who had heard and remembered my documentary and thought perhaps I might be the person they were seeking.

The war in Europe had ended, and the world's full attention was now on the Far East, where the army was fighting its way up through the Philippines toward Japan. The Red Cross public relations department had a man with them reporting Red Cross activities. His recordings were played over a group of U.S. radio stations known as the Associated Network, but apparently they were on the dull side. My job would be to take over and somehow liven up the program. I suggested making it a straight reporting job, not hard news—but of the human side of the GI experience, with unobtrusive plugs slipped in for the Red Cross.

They agreed. I would have carte blanche to travel with and live off the army and report on whatever interested me. A special arrangement was made for the American Broadcasting Company's Blue Radio Network to carry whichever of my stories appealed to them, on their Sunday News Roundup.

The only running role I had at that time was in the serial *Lorenzo Jones and His Wife Belle.* Organizing my affairs for my departure, I asked the Hummerts if they would, instead of replacing me, write the character out until I returned. Patriotically they agreed to do so.

Since I would officially be a Red Cross employee, I had to go the Washington headquarters for a physical examination and to fill out an application form.

The capital was full of amateur bureaucrats in those hectic days, and things often took a long time to go through "the works." I went back to New York and accepted radio acting jobs for the next five months, until word finally came that my application had been approved. I was to report immediately to Washington, where I would be given my embarkation orders.

Arriving in Washington, I was told that, although all my other papers were in order, my correspondent's accreditation had not yet come through and I would have to wait until it did. The wait lasted a few more months and stretched my patience to the breaking point.

I went back to New York several times to do a radio show, but since I was now in uniform and on the Red Cross payroll, I felt I owed them this time, even though I had been engaged only as an overseas radio correspondent. I offered my services to their publicity department.

They had me visit Red Cross installations and write up for their press releases stories about their activities in Washington hospitals, which at that time were crowded with war casualties. I vividly recall two of these occasions, to which I reacted strongly: one, with horror, as I went through a ward of hopeless basket cases, looking into the despairing eyes of these mute and totally helpless fragments of human beings; and later, in the recreation room, with hope—as I watched an audience of about fifty lesser paraplegics, mobile in wheelchairs, listening raptly to a concert by the Russian-born cellist, Piatagorsky. Most were ordinary GIs who had never attended a classical concert in their lives. You could feel the music strengthening them.

Although I managed to keep busy, the delay was terribly abrasive. I had already had my anti-malaria shots and was raring to go.

Then a funny thing happened on my way to the Philippines. The war ended. After all that waiting, General MacArthur pulled this fast one on me. On August 13, 1945, I had gone up to Baltimore on a visit. The next morning I was waiting on a busy corner for the return bus to Washington when news of the Japanese surrender hit the streets.

V-J Day! The end of World War II! I never saw such happiness! Pure, spontaneous, uninhibited joy. Delirious, screaming, shrieking, laughing, crying: people dancing in the streets. Strangers hugging each other; people piling over automobiles, moving and stationary. A cacophony of yelling, horn blowing, beating on dishpans, and the sirens of fire engines. Soldiers and sailors grabbed girls and

kissed them; soldiers and sailors kissed one another—girls
kissed soldiers and sailors: it was love, not war. After giving myself to it to the point of exhaustion, I jotted down
these snatches of remarks overheard:

AN ENGLISH SOLDIER: Never have I seen people exuding such
good will, not even on Christmas.
A YOUNG GIRL: I don't mind being kissed by someone my own
nationality. But this Frenchman grabbed me and kissed me till
I was ready to sock him before he let go.
AMERICAN SOLDIER: This is a happy day for me, all right. Just
came back from four years in the South Pacific.
ANOTHER SOLDIER: Look at these people, they're insane. I lost
two brothers in this war. I don't feel much like celebrating. Do
you know where there's a church that's open. I want to pray.

Instead of going to the Philippines, I was asked to go directly to Japan with the occupying troops, as soon as my
accreditation papers cleared MacArthur's press office—
which took another month, and even then only after the
Red Cross pulled some strings. MacArthur didn't want any
more correspondents with him. He didn't like them. They
made fun of his profile.

If I had been afraid flying to England in a bomber, it
was as nothing compared to my cowardice in crossing the
Pacific. This time too it was a bomber, but one that hadn't
been converted, thus much more uncomfortable. I was the
only passenger. The flight was divided into three large
chunks of fear. The first, somewhere in the black night between Seattle and Guam, occurred when one of the three-
man crew burst out of the cockpit with huge beads of
sweat on his forehead. Pushing me aside, he began to pull
up the floor boards of the fuselage. I asked what was the

matter. He didn't answer, but crawled down into the little compartment he had uncovered, and sniffed. "What's the matter?" I repeated, already terrified by his behavior. "Fire!" he said. "A red light on the dashboard has flashed fire!" I trembled so hard for the next half hour, as he sniffed out every inch of that plane, it's a wonder I didn't shatter my bones. I was worried; my life didn't flash before me the way it was supposed to. I had a few painful thoughts of my family, but it was mostly sheer tension and terror. I remember saying over and over to myself, "This is it, this is it," and speculating on the precise moment I would die when I became part of a flaming crash into the ocean. Finally, after several conferences, the crew decided the plane was not on fire, that a short circuit in the fire-reporting rheostat had caused the light to flash on. The pilot cut the wires so he wouldn't be faced with that blinking red light for the rest of the trip. Deliverance!

The next horror occurred hours later. The navigator told me to hang on to something and not be afraid. He wanted to experiment in determining his position by radar. He went back to the cockpit and the plane began a series of twists and turns, dips and steep pullouts that had me banging around from one end of the fuselage to the other. I grabbed some pipes running along the interior, but I wasn't prepared for these sudden, crazy maneuvers and lost my grip. "Don't be afraid," he said. Hah! Tell it to your subconscious. I ended up with new knots in my stomach, and a body of black and blue.

My third attack of fear came several hours out of Guam toward Tokyo, when I was honored by a visit from the pilot, a tall, slow-talking Texan.

"Listen," he said, "we're going to stop off in Iwo Jima.

If you're asked any questions, you don't know anything, okay?"

"Okay," I said, "but why: Aren't we supposed to fly direct to Tokyo?"

"Well," he drawled, "we just wanna pick up some cigarettes." He said he had radioed the airport that he had an emergency, and they had granted him permission to land. "We'll be going in on three engines," he said. "But don't be afraid."

"C-c-can you do that?" I asked, trying hard not to be afraid.

"Don't worry," he said. "I know my ship, I could even bring this baby in on two. We'll just be riding at a little different angle and have a heavier yaw."

With my nose to the window and my heart in my mouth, I watched him feather one propeller. The plane tilted heavily to one side. I fervently hoped his life was as precious to him as mine was to me. A crowd of soldiers, a crash car, and a fire engine were waiting as we touched down. The pilot modestly accepted congratulations for bringing the crippled plane down safely. He thoughtfully stroked his chin and made suggestions as to what could have happened. And as a team of mechanics pored over the conked-out engine he suggested we all have some chow. My God, I thought, what some people won't do for a cigarette.

After eating, I tagged along as the crew sauntered over to the PX, where they bought, not a pack or two of cigarettes, or even a carton or two. No. They bought as many cartons as they could hold in their arms and balance with their chins. Each carried away at least fifty cartons! What heavy smokers, I thought.

As we returned to the plane the mechanics were revving the motors. They simply hadn't been able to find what was wrong. They said everything was now working fine.

Back in the air, winging again toward Tokyo, I learned a lesson in Armed Forces' economics. I learned that not all the huge profits of war are made by armaments manufacturers and other giant corporations of the military-industrial complex. There's also room for the little fellow who does not have a lobbyist in Washington, or is not even particularly astute. He just has to be able to recognize an opportunity when it bangs on his door.

Take cigarettes, for instance. Cigarettes could buy anything in Japan. They were like legal tender, and the going price was thirty dollars a carton. At PXs, GIs were allowed to buy only two cartons a week for two dollars each. But on Iwo Jima they could buy as many as they wished for two dollars each. Iwo Jima was mostly a barren rock with no local populace willing to trade their goods and treasures for cigarettes, hence no need for the army to ration them. A made-to-order situation for these airmen. They had a very nice little thing going. Little? As I calculated, I realized it ran into big money: three of the airmen bought about fifty cartons each—150 cartons at two dollars apiece—at a cost of $300. In Japan, they would sell them for thirty dollars a carton, netting $4200. On one trip!

And they made three *scheduled* flights to Iwo Jima weekly. That was more than $50,000 a month. In six months they could clear over $300,000! God bless the law of supply and demand!

8. Welcome Honorable Enemy

My six months in Japan were a very different experience from my stay in England. In England I had
been in the midst of war, of bombing; here, although the
war was now over, the devastation of the cities was far
greater than London. Another surprise was our reception:
our deadly enemies, the great "yellow hordes" we had
been taught for years to fear and hate, had suddenly become our gracious hosts. The moment American troops set
foot on their home soil, the Japanese attacked with a barrage of politeness, deference, and eager cooperation for
which we were totally unprepared. It was strange and con-
fusing; surely some resistance was to be expected of a nation that produced 100,000 kamikaze suicide pilots and
had fought to the death for every inch of territory they
held in the South Pacific. But during my entire stay there
was not one reported act of violence to an American soldier. I never even encountered smoldering resentment.

The answer lay in the relationship of the Japanese to
their emperor—and in General MacArthur's understanding

127

of that relationship. There were great pressures to indict Hirohito as a war criminal, but MacArthur wisely decided—to the chagrin of liberals in the United States—to retain him as head of the nation, thereby unquestionably saving many thousands of lives. The people's profound reverence for their emperor became MacArthur's most effective tool in administering the occupation. Hirohito told his people to treat the Americans as guests, and they did. Japan was, undoubtedly, the most docile conquered country in history.

The Tokyo I arrived in in 1945 was not the bustling metropolis it is today. It was a city that gave you a feeling it almost wasn't there: miles of rubble, improvised shacks, and a small number of concrete buildings that had resisted the fire bombs rained down by our B-29s. The only vehicular traffic was army trucks and jeeps such as the one in which I was driven from Atsugi Airfield to the Dai Iti Hotel in the center of Tokyo where I was to stay, and a few rickshaws, pulled along by trotting humans. A dimly lighted street car, crammed with Japanese, rumbled by. Here and there policemen appeared, swinging lighted paper lanterns. Women in brightly colored kimonos, some with babies on their backs, were foraging in the rubble. Clusters of men, women, and children were sleeping on sidewalks, huddled around little fires. The weather was damp and penetrating, but many were barefooted and coatless.

The Dai Iti was a Western-style hotel, built expressly to house athletes at the Olympic Games which were to have taken place in Japan in 1940, but were canceled because of the war. As I registered, the desk sergeant asked my simulated rank. (I was wearing an officer's uniform with-

out insignia.) He must have liked me because when I told
him I didn't know, he said, "Only majors and colonels are
supposed to be billeted here, so I'll put you down as a colonel." From then on, whenever asked that question, I
always replied, "Colonel." In my travels throughout
Japan, it got me the best accommodations the army could
offer—food, transportation, chauffeurs, etc. I was forever
grateful to the Dai Iti desk sergeant for granting me my on-
the-spot commission.

My first meal in Japan was in the Dai Iti dining room. In
vivid contrast to the shambles just outside, it had a lovely,
luxurious ambience—flowers on every table, and overhead, flying free between the ledges of the high ceiling,
were finches, canaries, parakeets, and other small, exotic
songbirds. I was seated at a large round table with four
"real" American colonels. It was a good, stateside meal,
but unforgettable for the introductory remarks of our waitress. This lovely, virginal, kimonoed, Japanese lass, pencil poised to take our order, bowed, smiled, and said,
"American officers full of shit." There was a moment's
stunned silence at the table, which she quickly filled:
"Bullshit kiss my ass! What you have, prease?" Five very
perplexed Americans looked at one another until we rec-
ognized the heavy humor of some GI kitchen-worker who
had doubtless put her up to it, telling the girl, who obviously spoke little or no English, that it meant "good evening, it's a pleasure to serve you," or words to that effect.

Talk I overheard in the dining room and lobby indicated
the business of the occupation. The hotel was teeming
with military and civilian architects of Japan's future: a
couple of majors discussing a survey of Japan's lumber
resources; a woman member of a labor advisory commis-

sion telling a public relations officer how difficult it was to appraise the Japanese labor situation because of inflation; the recording secretary of the Allied Commission for governing Japan, explaining his job of keeping minutes of meetings and providing member nations with translated copies; a couple of legal minds tossing fine points of international law at each other in connection with the war criminal trials; a colonel from counterintelligence relating how his men had discovered a huge cache of diamonds in a Japanese attic; an elderly gentleman president of some waterworks in America, who had been sent to rectify flaws in the Japanese water system; an officer of the British Commonwealth Occupation Force discussing Japanese art with a French naval commander; a group of Russian Army officers talking in Russian about whatever Russian Army officers talk about in Russian.

Before retiring that night, I stepped outside for a stroll. I walked toward the only other building left standing in the immediate environment, Shinbashi Railroad Station. It was scorched, dirty, dimly lit, and unheated. As I entered, several hundred of Tokyo's dispossessed were settling down for the night on the cold floor. Their homes wiped out, they had no other place to go. Young and old, women in ragged, filthy kimonos, with sleeping babies on their backs, drooped their heads as they tried to doze in a kneeling position.

There was a sudden loud shriek. A woman appeared to be beating her small son with a stick as he lay, motionless, on the cold stone floor. Then I saw she was whacking the floor. I found a Japanese policeman and asked if he couldn't get the child to a hospital. He said all hospitals were so crowded only the police chief had the authority to do that. But he spoke a few words to the woman who told him her baby was not sick, just cold, that she was beating the floor so he wouldn't go to sleep and freeze. An old man crawled from his corner, peeled off one of his dirt-caked rags and placed it over the shivering boy.

I found a candy bar in my pocket and put it in the mother's hand. She rubbed my foot in gratitude. A number of people rose, and bowed deeply from the waist. This was to happen to me several times in Japan. Apparently when a foreigner shows a kindness to a native, even uninvolved witnesses thank him on behalf of the entire Japanese race.

The sun has a profound significance for the Japanese. Their Emperor is supposed to be a direct descendent of Amaterasu Omikami, the Sun Goddess, and the symbol of their flag is a round, blazing sun. As I left the station I found myself hoping the sun would return some of this devotion by shining the next day and shed a little warmth on some of these innocent victims of the war.

The following morning I checked in at Red Cross headquarters, then made my way through acres of ruins, toward Radio Tokyo, from which I was to broadcast my stories back to the United States. On my way down one of the meaningless streets, two small boys were playing baseball. A short distance away, hundreds of ragged human beings were milling about. Approaching, I saw it was an army garbage dump—practically a mess hall for these hungry people.

As I walked along parts of the ruins seemed to come alive—people were scrounging for bits of wood, metal, whatever building materials they could find. I was in the middle of a strange housing project. A scrawny little man, wearing army trousers and stripped to the waist, was shoveling debris away from a piece of wall. His wife, carrying an infant on her back, was dragging up several sheets of rusty tin that would be the roof of their new home. There were many homesteaders in this rubble wilderness, carving out patchwork hovels of their own. Several had planted gardens, and fresh vegetables were pushing their way up through the rubbish and broken masonry, as though Mother Nature were thumbing her nose at the efforts of Old Man Mars to wipe her out.

Radio Tokyo was the Radio City (village) of Japan: a medium-sized, six-story, modern building. Every inch of it smelled of fish. Every employee was either eating fish or had one stashed in his lunch box.

There were signs at all entrances: OFF LIMITS FOR ALL ALLIED MILITARY PERSONNEL NOT ON OFFICIAL BUSINESS. But there was plenty of official business, army khaki swarming all over the place.

I explored their facilities with great curiosity. Most of the radio equipment was as modern as ours, although run down. There were sixteen studios, all modern with a single exception: one was designed like a Japanese living room, with Tatami mats on the floor and a small, low round table. The performer would take his shoes off before entering, and broadcast while kneeling on a cushion. This was the studio from which the famous American renegade known as Tokyo Rose had used her sexy voice to try and demoralize and seduce GIs into deserting. Now it was being used by an American actor, Hans Conried, for a humorous chatter program he called *Tokyo Mose*, broadcast over the Armed Forces Network, which shared these facilities. Armed Forces Radio also rebroadcast many popular programs from home, such as *Information, Please! Edgar Bergen and Charlie McCarthy, Suspense,* The Detroit Symphony, and an occasional Norman Corwin show.

American radio stations had some strange-looking gadgets in their sound-effects closets, but some of Radio Tokyo's effects were among the most inventive I've ever seen. Cricket noises were made by rubbing the backs of two small seashells together. Rain was achieved by gently shaking from side to side two large, round fans to which about thirty small dried beans were attached, each by a two-inch length of string. For the putt-putt of a motor boat, the sound-effects man clamped his hand on and off the end of a hollow piece of bamboo. There were several resonant gongs, which play an important part in all Oriental drama, and an enormous seashell with a mouthpiece attached, which, when blown into, produced an unearthly sound used for God knows what.

The head engineer, Kazuichi Fuigi, informed me that throughout the Japanese Isles, aside from 150,000-watt Radio Tokyo, there were eight 10,000-watt stations, twenty-five 500-watt, and fifty smaller ones. The bombings had knocked out line communications between many of them, but they carried network programs via shortwave. There were an estimated 7,000,000 home radio sets in use at that time.

A set owner paid a government tax of one yen per month—a little over six cents, at the then current rates.

All programs began at six in the morning, and all stations signed off at ten-thirty at night.

The Allied authorities had revised Radio Tokyo's program schedules to include round-table discussions, audience participation shows, and especially encouraged listeners to break through their traditional submission to authority by writing letters to the station expressing their own opinions and desires. The reticent Japanese had responded en masse: thousands of letters had poured in. I glanced through some of them, which had been translated—often literally—for the occupying authorities.

Please play light music and story ending in a joke. We live in cold dwelling, so if we can hear interesting drolleries on cold winter night—we hoping to distract our minds by radio.

We like to hear about reconstruction—especially Hiroshima. I think radio is organ of education as well as amusement.

Thank you. My father likes to hear "The Story of Dutiful Child of Snow with Moon."

Your program used to impregnate Japanese minds with American ideas. I don't know how much salary you radio people are receiving, but these hypocritical broadcasts only irritate the people. Let Americans take care of their own propaganda. Are you endeavoring to trample the utterly exhausted people until they become a fourth-rate nation? Do you attempt to make second Philippines out of Japan?

I desire to have radio plays suitable for farmers. I think jokes are most suitable to distract one's mind. Also old story.

Day by day it is getting cold. I like to hear music of friendly Japan and United States please.

I like answer for following questions: What is composition of humans and animals? Water colors? Why snow has certain formation? Why leaves fall from trees? Why can see your breath only in the morning? Why United States people taller than us?

I desire solos on Japanese instrument. Its beautiful sounds in quiet cold long evening makes us forget we are struggling for living.

I would like to hear reading of works by famous poets. Also love songs for girls.

For those of us who farm in countryside, western music makes us dizzy and dull. We sincerely hope you will broadcast more Japanese music.

I would like to hear dramatized biographies of famous chemists.

Please teach to us something make us cheerful. National song.

We like to be like GI but don't have enough politeness. Rather, what we have is false. Please have radio program to develop our real social politeness.

In these days with shortages of food, why are so many factories on arable land that should be allotted for rice fields? The factories and smaller cities should be removed to the mountains.

We have begun aiming at highly civilized level necessary for the moral nation. New leaders of Japan should not be same persons as those who acclaim the militarism.

I appeal to the authorities for immediate removal of licensed prostitution. It should be immediately abolished for the elevation of women's position.

How about evening with samisen? I think that would be suitable on cold nights.

When I was middle-school boy, I hated most the course in morals—because the Emperor was unreasonably revered as living God. Feeling it was not right, I was always in great mental agony and seized with great fear. But today I am in a rebellious mood, thanks to Supreme Command of Allied Powers who arranged that we can freely criticize the Emperor System.

The movies of our country should be made by more civilized hands with much poetic spirit, instead of pursuing American nation.

The letters seemed to focus on two major points: the compulsion to escape into old stories, sweet songs, and bright jokes that would distract them from their misery, and a tentative acceptance of their new freedom to criticize their leaders without fear of the notorious Thought Police.

But even though the letters showed that, behind all the agreeable smiles and bows, the Japanese had all the hungers, fears, hopes, and confused emotions of a scrutable westerner, their preoccupation with "face" made it difficult for the occupation forces to establish a working relationship with the population. For one thing, the Japanese would generally answer questions affirmatively, say yes when they really meant no. But it wasn't lying as we know it. It was a ritual politeness—even with each other—to say what they thought you wanted to hear, communicating the truth behind the words in subtle, nonverbal ways endemic to their culture, and difficult if not impossible for foreigners to understand.

Roaming around the country, I found so much that was strange and difficult to understand that, in the three minutes allotted me for each of my five weekly broadcasts, I decided simply to describe what I saw and experienced; rather than attempt any heavy interpretations or analyses, I made up my mind to create a picture of the life of this unique occupation through a mosaic of vignettes.

Norman Corwin had given me the address of a Japanese friend to look up. After driving my jeep through miles of devastation, I arrived at a small, unpretentious Japanese home in the suburbs of Tokyo. I was greeted at the door by Yoichi Hiroaka, the world-famous xylophonist. He had lived in the United States for twelve years and had been a featured soloist with the New York Philharmonic, the NBC Symphony under Toscanini, and other prominent orchestras.

A small, ebullient man of about forty, with bright gleaming eyes behind heavy double-lensed glasses, he invited me to take off my shoes and come in. He introduced me to his pretty American-born wife, and, as my hands warmed around the cup of hot tea she set in front of me, Hiroaka told me his story.

Before the war he had been doing very well in the United States. His musicianship was lauded and appreciated by the country's foremost critics. Then came Pearl Harbor. Immediately, all his concert dates were cancelled and he was barred from all network radio programs. The problem of making a living for his wife and baby became acute. His fellow musicians took up a collection for him, but it didn't last long.

"There was absolutely no way for me to support my family in America," he said. "The government had begun to round up all Japanese—even the American-born—and put them in an internment camp. I reluctantly chose to return to Japan on an exchange ship."

I asked him about life under the B-29s, and he said, "How we lived through that hell I'll never know. This is our third house. We were bombed out of the other two. And the noise those incendiaries made—like a steady torrent of rain. And they were loaded with some devilish stuff that prevented you from being able to extinguish the fires. Since I arrived from the United States, I've lost thirty-five pounds, from 140 to 105."

I asked what effect the war had on music in Japan. "I'll

tell you this," he said. "The sound those whistling fire bombs made was in the key of G. Whenever my wife strikes a G-note on our piano, we still jump out of our skins."

Bouncing along in my jeep back toward the hotel, suddenly I saw in the glare of my headlights a young, kimonoed girl. She was standing in the middle of the road, frantically waving her arms. I jammed on the brakes, and she ran over to me, screaming and pointing to a U.S. Army weapons carrier parked in the shadows on the side of the road. I caught a glimpse of several GIs quickly ducking behind it.

"Get in!" I shouted to her, pointing over my shoulder to the back seat. "Quick!"

She climbed in, pounded me on the back and yelled "Friendo! Friendo!"

I gathered the GIs were still holding the girl's friend, whom she wanted me to rescue too. But I wasn't about to tangle with a nest of horny rapists on a lonely highway in the middle of the night. That's for the movies. I stepped on the gas and cut away at full speed.

But my passenger continued hysterical, crying and jabbering in a Japanese interspersed with an occasional "Friendo, friendo!" as she continued pounding me on the back. Unfortunately I couldn't make her understand I was not John Wayne, or convince her how lucky she was I had been able to rescue her. My heroism was based on an instant calculation that my jeep could travel faster than a weapons carrier.

I was wrong. Just as I began to relax, I became aware of two large, hostile headlights reflected in my rear view mirror. I stepped on the gas. The distance between us didn't change. I pushed down on the accelerator as hard as I dared on that rubble-strewn road—we were already leaping along semi-airborne—but the headlights grew larger. It became painfully clear that I couldn't outrace them, so I slammed on the brakes and came to a screeching stop. Beside the road was a sparsely-wooded area with a thick underbrush. The girl was still sobbing as I pulled her out of the jeep and pushed her toward the woods. She misunderstood my motives and again began to panic. I pointed to the rapidly approaching truck, then to the woods, and pantomimed for her to run like hell. She finally caught on and scurried into the brush.

I climbed back in the jeep just as the big weapons carrier swung around in front of me to cut off my escape and stopped. For a long moment no one made a move. I heard muffled sobs—evidently emanating from the "friend." I sat stiffly, waiting for them to come at me. My heart was pounding. "At last," I thought, "you're going to experience the horror of war . . . at the hands of your own countrymen!" But the soldiers were cautious. After all, I might be a high officer. You never know who's driving a jeep. One of the men finally got out and ambled over, squinting to get a better look at me. I was wearing an officer's cap and uniform, but when he came close enough to see I was without insignia—a lousy civilian—he made a disgusted face and signaled the others. Five or six glowering, Texas-tall GIs moved in on me.

"What the fuck's the idea highjackin' our girl?" the first one said.

"Where is she?" another demanded.

"Look," I said, "the girl was scared to death . . ."

"What the fuck's it to you?"

"Where the fuck is she?"

"She was hysterical," I said. "She could have died of heart failure. There are plenty of girls around the Ginza, why do you want to pick on a . . ."

"What the fuck's it your business?"

"Where is she?"

"She musta beat it inta the woods."

"C'mon, let's fan out."

"All right you—get the fuck outa here!"

I did. As this splendid unit of brave American soldiers fanned out in the tall underbrush to flush out their quarry—one desperately frightened little Japanese girl.

While every army has its share of monsters, there were relatively few such incidents during the occupation. Japanese women, trained to believe their highest mission in life was to serve, flatter and entertain men, charmed most GIs into their best behavior.

And, while the majority of American males may be chauvinist pigs at heart, their patronizing politeness to women actually gave a big nudge to the meager women's liberation movement in Japan. This may sound like Women's Lib in reverse, but the smiles of Japanese women had a little extra charge when for the first time in their lives they experienced the seductive pleasure of a man holding a door open for them, or giving them a seat on a crowded trolley. It was new and ego-strengthening—and a severe shock to the Japanese male, accustomed to his God-given right of preceding his woman through a door, and, if there's only one empty seat on the trolley, occupying it himself, leaving her to stand—frequently with an infant on her back.

During the war, the women's movement in Japan took a big step forward, as hundreds of thousands of women went to work in factories, taking over men's occupations. But the male power structure was very deeply rooted in the culture, and the vast majority of women had no revolutionary passion to overthrow it. Even when they sympathized with the notion of equality and democracy, their reactions were often bizarre, as I was soon to see.

One day I ran into an actor I had known in New York, Al Lipton, who was now a private in the occupying army producing radio shows for the Armed Forces Network. Al was also a passionate believer in democracy for everyone, including women, and did a little missionary work on behalf of the cause whenever he could. In the course of his proselytizing, he voiced his views one day to a Japanese gentleman named Mr. Cho. He told Mr. Cho how strongly he felt that the remaining remnants of feudalism should be abolished in Japan.

Mr. Cho, who happened to be president of a Japanese press association, thought it would be a fine idea if Private Lipton would speak at the next meeting of his organization, whose members would be most eager to hear a GI's impressions of Japan. Al accepted the invitation on the spot.

A few days later Al spoke for an hour and a half at the press-association meeting, explaining why he felt the defeat of Japanese militarism was actually a victory for the Japanese people. He spoke of the need to reorganize the country along democratic lines, and especially stressed the importance of having women assert their rights and play a meaningful role in civic and social life. "Women have too long been considered inferior," he said, "mere chattel."

He pointed to the struggles and ultimate victories of American suffragettes, and finished his speech by urging the women of Japan to take full advantage of their new opportunity to vote, as their first major battle in a campaign to shed the chains of their ancient feudal bondage and recover their rights and dignity as human beings.

The speech made an extraordinary impression. Afterward the audience gathered around, shook Al's hands, applauded, and bowed in double time.

As a result of that talk, Private Lipton was later the guest of honor at a special dinner. The food served was the best that could be bought on the black market: rice wrapped in smoked and raw fish, clam broth, broiled sparrows, sukiyaki, and pear preserves. Wine, beer, and hot sake were served with every course.

After dinner, Lipton was approached by a middle-aged Japanese lady wearing a beautiful, crested silk kimono. She explained, in her slight English, how much she liked what he had said, especially about freedom for women. As a token of her appreciation she would like to make him a little present. She left the room and returned shortly with a beautiful young Japanese girl. Pressing her gently toward Lipton, she said, bowing, "Presento—for you—to keep." She had just bought the girl from her father for a couple of thousand yen, to show her appreciation of his speech on freedom for Japanese women.

Lipton blinked five or six times, then realized his plight. It would be terrible manners to refuse the gift—a downright insult, in fact. He tried to change the subject, but his admirers just smiled. He took his wallet from his pocket and pointed to a photograph. "Wifeoo-babee—Columbus, Ohio," he said. But they kept on smiling, noting that, indeed, his wife was very pretty. Only when he told them he lived in a barracks and had no place to keep such a "presento" did they reluctantly withdraw the gift. The barracks' problem was a practical consideration, and therefore no "face" was lost.

"I can see it's going to take a long time to educate Japanese women about freedom," said Private Lipton. "Either that, or I made a lousy speech."

The Japanese are probably the world's greatest present-givers. But it's not always an expression of total generosity. One day not long after Al Lipton's speech, a young Japanese acquaintance rushed up to me, gave me that one, one-two bow, elaborately apologized for disturbing me, and thrust a small wooden box into my hand. I opened it and found, wrapped in heavy cotton, a delicately carved ivory figure: a netsuke, with inlaid metal and semi-precious stones.

"What's this?" I asked.

"Presento," he said, with a big grin. "Presento from my father. He want you have this for Christmas."

"But I've never met your father," I protested.

"All same, he want you have nice Christmas," he replied.

I handed it back to him and said that he should tell his father I was very moved, but that I had done nothing to deserve such a valuable gift.

"Oh, it is all right," said the young man. "You keep. My father would like American cigarette."

How profoundly the American occupation changed the bases of relationships between men and women in Japan is a question for sociologists to sort out; but it did a great deal to break up the totalitarian structure of Japan's social, economic, and political life.

One of the first things Hirohito did was to democratize himself. He launched a campaign to divest himself of his divinity. He put on a beat-up old felt hat and made a lot of public appearances. American correspondents helped the new image along by calling him "Charlie."

In the past people had had to draw their curtains when the Emperor's procession passed through the streets. It was a crime to look "down" upon him. One day I traveled with Hirohito as he visited a project for bombed-out victims. He spoke a few words to a couple of women, who were so overcome they burst into tears.

Under MacArthur's prodding, the formation of free labor unions was energetically encouraged. Even Hirohito's palace guards began presenting demands. Organizations all over the country undertook to "democratize" themselves, including the Sumo Wrestlers Federation.

The rickshaw men of Tokyo reacted collectively when the American authorities posted traffic signs: SPEED—30 MILES PER HOUR. They descended on MacArthur's headquarters to protest they couldn't run that fast.

The unions also came up with some original strike techniques. The streetcar workers, in order to hit at their bosses without inconveniencing the public, let the public ride free. When this didn't work, they collected the fares, took out their wage increase, and turned in what was left to the company.

The telephone workers reinforced their demands by cutting off all calls to and from the executives of the company. On all public calls the operator would say, "This company is unfair to us they do not pay us living wage number please?"

But perhaps the most innovative and cathartic of all was the "shriek" strike. When the railroad workers were demanding more money, at a certain, exact time every day, all over the country every employee—blue and white collar alike—would stop whatever he was doing and shriek for about three minutes at the top of his lungs, the idea being to call public attention to their situation, and make the employer lose face.

Sometimes "democracy" got a little out of hand. I met a professor named Hatano, who told me that, during one of his lectures at Tokyo University, a student rose and started to leave. When asked where he was going, he said, "Home." Hatano told him to wait until the lecture was over. "No, sir," he replied. "I exercise my democratic privilege to do what I please."

Hatano introduced me to a number of interesting people, who provided good material for my broadcasts. One was a Frenchman named Jean-Pierre Hochcorne, who had lived in Japan for fifteen years. Prior to the war he had been an employee of the French Consulate; when the war broke out he was interned. He had a particularly brutal guard whose pastime was jamming bamboo splinters under his fingernails and trying to beat him into confessing he was a spy. His cell was on the ground floor and its window faced the street. His wife brought him food, handing it through the bars, but he was not permitted to speak to her. So they developed a way of communicating by barking like dogs. Three rapid barks meant one thing, one short and one long meant something else, and so forth. When the guard threatened punishment, Monsieur

Hochcorne convinced him the prison rules only forbade speaking, not barking.

Professor Hatano came to visit me one day in my hotel room as I was about to leave for dinner. He brought along a friend, whom he introduced as Japan's most famous mystery writer, Edagowa Rampo. Stare at the name for a moment. It's the Japanese way of pronouncing Edgar Allan Poe.

I asked him if readers didn't confuse him with the real Edgar Allan Poe, who was also published there. "Oh, no," Hatano replied. "Ours is much more famous."

After some broad hinting, the reason for their visit became clear. They were hungry. Food was scarce in Tokyo.

I told them to wait in my room while I went down to dinner. I stuffed most of it, and a large second helping of chicken, under my Eisenhower jacket and brought it back up to them.

Edagowa Rampo was so grateful he came to visit me again, to present me with several rare, old, gruesome Japanese prints, which he said he collected against his will. Then he asked if I would do him another little favor when I got back to the States. Would I mail him all the Agatha Christie mysteries published in America during the war?

It set me to wondering just how he became such a famous mystery writer. But no . . . I shall give him the benefit of the doubt.

Still I kept wondering how Agatha Christie would be pronounced in Japanese.

9. Hiroshima

I felt I had to do a broadcast on Hiroshima. The atomic bomb had fallen only eight weeks before and the city was still off-limits to most army personnel. Through the Red Cross, however, I wangled a permit. It was the most awesome experience of my life. Hiroshima was still one big, quivering, raw wound.

As I drove my jeep uncertainly through the rubble, I was approached by a small man on a bicycle, who introduced himself as the Reverend Kioshi Tanimoto, pastor of Hiroshima's Central Methodist Church. He offered to show me around. But first he had heard that a sick parishioner of his was living somewhere in the ruins and he was bringing him a piece of dried fish, would I care to come along? We searched for half an hour until we found a weak old man and his son—all that was left of a family of nine—living in a small lean-to improvised from the wreckage. They gratefully accepted the fish and bowed their heads to the ground. I gave each a cigarette, which he smoked ecstatically. Then a dismayed expression came over their faces as they looked about the miserable hovel for a gift for me. It's a Japanese custom for the host to give his visitor a present. But here there was nothing. Suddenly the son's face brightened. From behind a pile of charred wood, he pulled out a rusty old American saxophone, stepped outside where he could straighten up, and there in the midst of all that atomic devastation, played, for my pleasure, "My Blue Heaven" and "I'll Buy That Dream." Whenever I remember those soulful notes floating among the ruins of Hiroshima, I'm still shaken.

Tanimoto took me to Hiroshima's Red Cross hospital— one of the few buildings left standing—where Dr. Fumio Shigeto, the assistant director, showed us around.

It was badly seared, and the windows were almost glass-less. The white plaster walls of the rooms were pock-marked with holes from flying glass. In one room blood was spattered all over the walls and ceiling; the blast had blown the window into the face of a patient and severed an artery.

Dr. Shigeto told me that twenty-one of the hospital's nurses were killed, and of the thousands who managed to reach the hospital that first day, over 700 had died. Many who couldn't quite make it were found dead on the grounds outside.

On the hospital's outer wall, a horizontal series of red splotches abruptly turned into a downward smear just short of the entrance—mutely telling the story of a bloody hand groping toward help until it could no more.

Most of the in-patients had suffered fractures and internal injuries when their houses fell on them. Thousands died from blood disease. Dr. Shigeto told me that many of them might have been saved by transfusions, but the blood of practically everyone in Hiroshima had been affected to some degree, so there was no healthy blood available for transfusions.

We went to a room where a long line of out-patients was being treated. One woman's arms were gnarled strips of purple flesh. Her nine-year-old daughter was almost bald. Many people had lost all their hair after the explosion, but eyebrows, strangely, had not been affected.

One man had severe burns on the back of his neck. Although there was a concrete wall between him and the explosion, the intense rays had bounced off a building in back of him and struck him from behind. A nurse was treating these patients with zinc ointment. She turned, and I saw that half of her face was burned away.

Dr. Shigeto told me that he was the first person in Japan to realize what had happened. "The papers simply called it a new type of bomb," he said, "but when I unpacked some negative film for an X-ray machine and found it had completely degenerated, I knew immediately it had been destroyed by the gamma rays of an atomic bomb."

A number of American doctors had visited the hospital to study chemical reactions of victims and the possibilities of treatment.

"I hope they'll never have to make use of their knowledge," Dr. Shigeto said grimly.

When I told Dick Day, Tokyo head of Red Cross Public Relations, that I planned to do a series of broadcasts on Hiroshima, he advised against it. "No one wants to hear about Hiroshima any more," he said. "It's old stuff."

But I felt that so far most, if not all the reporting had been of numbers: how many tens of thousands killed; the

damage at various distances from the center of the explosion, etc. Statistics for the military manuals and history
books. After what I had witnessed and what Tanimoto had
told me of his and others' experiences, it seemed much
more important that the story of Hiroshima be told and
remembered in terms of human agony.

I spread my material over three of my three-minute
broadcasts, but I couldn't begin to encapsulate my feelings, or the suffering of the people of Hiroshima, in this
meager air time. Nevertheless, I described as best I could
the old man, the son and the saxophone; Dr. Shigeto and
the Red Cross Hospital. And more.

On February 16, 1946, I broadcast my story of the Reverend Kioshi Tanimoto's nightmare day:

JOSEPH JULIAN

ASSOCIATED NETWORK BROADCAST

WAR CORRESPONDENT

JANUARY 16, 1946

GHQ PRO

This is Joseph Julian, your Red Cross correspondent speaking
from Tokyo.

The Reverend Kioshi Tanimoto, American-educated pastor of
Hiroshima's Central Methodist church, invited me to his home
for a cup of tea. His church had been leveled by the atom
bomb and he now rents a house on the outskirts of the ruins. In
one of the rooms he has improvised an altar and conducts services every morning for about twenty surviving members of his
congregation.

He poured the tea and said grace beginning with "Oh Lord
we thank thee for being alive." Never was a prayer said less ritually or with more honest fervor.

And as we squatted there on the straw matted floor sipping
our "ocha" he told me his story of that day. He was visiting

friends just outside the city, he said. "About twelve noon, I heard a terrific roar, and the house I was in began to shake. I thought it was an ordinary air raid, until I went outside. It was dark as night—fires were everywhere and thousands of people were pouring across bridges from Hiroshima. It was like the end of the world. I didn't know what happened, but I knew it was something catastrophic. My first thought was for my wife and baby girl who were in our house on the other side of town. I tried to get across several bridges, but the fires were too hot. I ran four miles along the river that circles the city proper. Then I swam across. There were at least a thousand people lying on the beach. It was difficult to walk without stepping on them. I met a friend who told me my wife and child had been buried in the collapse of our house, but had dug their way to safety. Most of those wounded lying on the beach kept asking for water. I found a broken dish and scooped water from the river and gave hundreds of them a little swallow each. River water is bad but I hoped it would help them psychologically. Almost all of them thanked me and bowed before they drank the water— even though they were dying. I worked with them for several hours, doing what I could. Then the tide came in and washed many of them into the river. I pulled five dead bodies out of an old row boat and rescued about twenty people. Some would hold up their arms to be pulled into the boat, but their burns were so raw when I grabbed them, they couldn't stand the pain and jerked away—to drown."

The heroic little pastor went on to describe the equally terrifying experiences of his friends, then interrupted himself, saying he was sorry but he had to keep an appointment with a Buddhist priest and a Hiroshima businessman. They were to meet at a designated spot in the ruins to discuss raising money to build a monument.

"What kind of a monument?" I asked.

"It will serve several purposes," he replied. "There are bones of entire families in the ruins, with no one to bury them. We are going to collect them into a common grave at the foot of the monument. It will comfort the spirit of the dead. And, according to the Emperor, the bomb on Hiroshima helped end the war. Therefore, most of the people here feel their suffering was not in vain. This will be a monument to their sacrifice."

I asked him what the inscription would be.

"We have not yet decided on the exact wording," he answered, "but it will certainly contain our prayer for eternal peace."

This is Joseph Julian in Tokyo. I return you now to the Associated Network.

My broadcasts from a small studio in Radio Tokyo were beamed to San Francisco, where I was recorded for later airing over the Associated Network and the American Broadcasting Company's *Sunday News Roundup*. But as I signed off these Hiroshima spots, I received calls on the two-way radio from operators at island outposts all over the South Pacific. They had tuned in and felt bound to tell me immediately how deeply the Hiroshima stories had moved them.

For the next few months I continued to send back little pieces of the mosaic:

The hissing sound some Americans find so offensive in Japanese speech is really a form of politeness. By sucking in air through their teeth they demonstrate they are not forcing their own breath on you.

Japanese farmers are extremely skillful. Americans are constantly amazed at the weird agricultural goings-on, such as fresh vegetables pushing up through snow fields, and oranges growing in the dead of winter.

When a Japanese woman goes shopping she knows what to do with baby—bundle it on her back, leaving her hands free to examine merchandise and do her share of shoving at a bargain counter. The GIs call them the "two-headed women."

Probably the world's most unique firefighting equipment is housed in Minami Temple, in Osaka. It consists of about 200 huge bamboo fans. Whenever a fire breaks out anywhere in the vicinity, parishioners flock to the temple, where, together with priests, they each grab a fan, climb to the roof, disperse themselves along the perimeter, and fan like mad to keep flying sparks away.

But the Hiroshima experience had dampened my enthusiasm for these low-keyed vignettes. Besides, I had been in Japan about five months now and was about ready to head home.

I returned to the United States on an LST troopship. If I'm ever asked to play the role of a sardine I'll have an in-depth understanding of the part. I've never been in such tight proximity to so many human beings over such a long period of time. I was told there were five thousand GIs and officers jammed on that ship. I was billeted with the officers, who had slightly more *Lebensraum* than the GIs; still, about twenty of us were stacked in four-tier bunks in a very small area. And even though it was a homecoming and spirits and forebearance were unusually high, my first few days on the cramped eleven-day journey were pretty oppressive. Then I made a wonderful discovery. I found a tiny, unused room on the top forward deck. It contained some cleaning materials and a desk and chair and it was unlocked. It became a sanctuary where I could be alone whenever I wished. But more important, that desk inspired me to write a play. I called it *Presento* and it was based on the situation of my friend, Al Lipton, and his unexpected "gift." By the end of the voyage I had finished the first act. It took me three years to write the rest. Confinement seems to be good for writer's block.

10. Return to New York

Back in New York I merged my three Hiroshima radio spots into an article and offered it to an agent for marketing. *Déjà vu*.

"Hiroshima's old stuff," she said. "No one wants to hear about that any more."

No one except millions of people. A few months later John Hersey's book *Hiroshima* was published. He explored the city after I was there, and had put together a book of six first-person narratives—six individuals describing their personal experience of the bomb. It created a sensation.

The New York *Herald Tribune* published this "old stuff" in its entirety; the *New Yorker* gave over a whole issue to the book, and the American Broadcasting Company decided to do a straight reading of Hersey's *Hiroshima* as a special one-hour program over its network.

Six radio actors were called to do the reading, one for each of the six stories. Coincidentally I was one of the six chosen. Even more incredible, the story I was assigned to read was that of the Reverend Kioshi Tanimoto.

I didn't resent having to read Hersey's report of Tanimoto's experience. His book, of course, presented it in much greater detail than I had been able to. I welcomed any opportunity available to render Hiroshima human, to counteract its being compressed into a paragraph of cold statistics. Today's bombs are a thousand times more powerful: the horror of Hiroshima multiplied a thousand times. After having seen with my own eyes what that one "tiny" bomb had done, I knew the full meaning of the expression, "the end of the world." It used to be an empty cliché; it isn't any more.

I put together a half-hour radio documentary of my experiences that I couldn't deal with fully in my short broadcasts from Tokyo. I peddled it to an organization called The United World Federalists, and it was presented over WJZ and its affiliates on March 13, 1947. The introductory pages went like this:

VOICE: These are the words of Socrates: "When you are asked your country, never reply, 'I am an Athenian,' or 'I am a Corinthian,' but—'I am a citizen of the universe!' "

ANNOUNCER: This is the *World Security Workshop*, presented by the American Broadcasting Company and United World Federalists, to help Americans understand the way ahead to lasting peace, and to offer evidence that all peoples can, in truth, become citizens of the universe.

SOUND: (*Establish busy street: traffic, passers-by, etc. Hold under:*)

JULIAN: Pardon me, could you tell me how to get to Shinbashi Railroad Station?

JAPANESE: Wakareemasen. . . ?

JULIAN: Oh . . . uh . . . Shinbashi . . . uh . . . tayeesha-bawa . . . uh . . . doko deska?

JAPANESE: Ah so deska! Ima wakaramashta. Mingee dess-heedayreedes-matsoongoo sakedess.

JULIAN: Okay, thank you . . . uh . . . aringato!

SOUND: (*Hold street pattern, then fade under*)

ANNOUNCER: This is Roger Krupp. Tonight, as the eighteenth in its series of original scripts, the *World Security Workshop* departs from its usual form to present a special program, "Welcome, Honorable Enemy!" The voice you just heard asking the direction of Tokyo's Shinbashi Railroad Station, is that of Joseph Julian, who is well known to radio as an actor. Mr. Julian recently returned from a tour of Japan, where he was sent as a special correspondent. The impressions he gathered, the appraisal he made of the postwar Japanese, and the opinions he formed about our responsibilities to this conquered people, were so interesting to us of the *World Security Workshop* that we felt our audience should hear them. The atomic age has conferred a larger citizenship upon all of us. Whether we like it or not, we are now *world* citizens. World security can be achieved only if we become *good* world citizens, and that means enlarging our understanding of the problems of every country in the world. One of the vital problems that today faces us in the United States is how to insure the transformation of a once potent aggressor into a peace-loving member of the family of nations. As a report on conditions there, with which our occupation forces must cope in achieving this objective, Joseph Julian has written, "Welcome, Honorable Enemy!"

I developed an original format that allowed me to hang the show on an interview. The announcer asked me questions, I gave a short reply, then we'd fade into a dramatization that would illustrate my point. There was no music, just a large cast and many sound-effects.

John Crosby, then radio critic of the New York *Herald*

Tribune, wrote a column reviewing the radio reading of Hersey's *Hiroshima* and, again a coincidence, in the same column, my own documentary, "Welcome, Honorable Enemy!" I quote it at length because it shows the high level of criticism that obtained in those heydays and nights of radio, and because it also has a number of pregnant things to say about the techniques of radio.

Radio in Review
By John Crosby

There was a story in the early days of broadcasting, probably apocryphal, about a sound-effects man who was seriously frustrated in his attempts to reproduce the sound of clashing swords. He tried rolling a barrel full of tin cans, he experimented vainly with the sound of splashing water, but neither these nor a dozen other devices sounded at all right. Finally, in desperation, he tried clashing two swords together. It worked fine.

Writers in trying to convey information in plain news or in documentary broadcasts have pursued somewhat the same course: that is, they will go to preposterous lengths to avoid simply telling the information. With great and frequently misspent ingenuity, they have employed drama, massed choirs, street noises, crowd noises, symphony orchestras, and sometimes, when absolutely necessary, the sound of the human voice.

Of course it would be foolish to carry the analogy too far. Much of this experiment in the art of sound, if such a phrase is permissible, has been strikingly effective in putting across an idea, or, in some cases, just a plain news story. Still, in looking back upon a great many documentary broadcasts of one sort or another, the most effective one I ever heard was the braodcast of John Hersey's *Hiroshima* over the American Broadcasting Company. At the insistence of Hersey, who resisted all attempts to have the story dramatized, *Hiroshima* was simply read. The only concession to broadcasting technique was the employment of different voices for the various parts of the story devoted to the six different characters.

This method transmitted to the listener not only the highly dramatic story but also the keen intelligence that went into its writing. The listener was left with the impression of a gifted mind assembling the fragments of one of the most significant stories of our time. If the screams of the dying or the crackle of flames had been allowed to intrude, the braodcast would have descended to the level of all the broadcasts which have ever used these sounds, including a great many whodunits.

Recently, the American Broadcasting Company presented another highly effective, but somewhat different documentary called, "Welcome, Honorable Enemy!" on its series of public service broadcasts called *World Security Workshop*. "Welcome, Honorable Enemy!" presented impressions of occupied Japan of Joseph Julian, a radio actor who formerly broadcast for the Red Cross in Japan.

The technique, I should say, was about halfway between the *Hiroshima* reading and the traditional method. Julian used a good deal of straight drama, but he also used far more than the normal amount of plain exposition. The exposition took the form of a conversation between Julian and his announcer, Roger Krupp. Somehow, the two men sounded as relaxed as if they were discussing Japan over an after-dinner cup of coffee and at the same time the talk had the coherence of a well-written script.

Julian explained why the Japanese did all that hissing, how illogical the Japanese are about their emperor, and what a shriek strike is. Along with each small anecdote he interpolated his own serious interpretation. By avoiding both clichés and pretension, the two men succeeded in sounding intelligent, one of the most difficult things in the world to do over the air.

The trick, I guess, is to match the technique to the message. To employ an ear-catching device when you are attempting to engage the intelligence is a serious mistake in anatomy. It is not sounds that stir men's minds, but ideas, and the sounds employed to put the ideas across ought to be on the same intellectual level as the ideas.

Radio dramas were still in full flower when I returned from Japan in March, 1946, although the upstart, television, was beginning to nibble at radio's space on the entertainment pages.

Before I left for Japan, television was still very crude. On June 30, 1944, actress Leslie Woods and I had played the leads in a short, two-character play, *The Favor*. It was the first drama ever televised by CBS. Their single camera was stationary. Thus only one set could be used, and no close-ups were possible. Mobile television cameras had not yet been developed. Worthington Minor, a Broadway stage director, was in charge of the production. After the telecast he had invited us to his apartment to view the first, televised professional boxing match. There were only about three hundred video sets in New York at the time, and the reception was so fuzzy, the only way we could distinguish the two fighters was by the light and dark colors of their trunks.

Now, almost two years later, television had improved, but it still couldn't begin to compete with radio and its cornucopia of programming and high-salaried entertainers. Americans were still laughing at the jokes of The Great Gildersleeve, Edgar Bergen, Jack Benny, Jack Haley, Eddie Cantor, Amos 'n' Andy, Abbott and Costello, Bob Burns, Henny Youngman, Bob Hope, and Burns and Allen. They were dancing to the big band jazz of Harry James, Duke Ellington, Tommy Dorsey, and Sammy Kaye; they were being beguiled by the close harmony of the

Andrews Sisters and the sweet sounds of Sinatra, Crosby, Lena Horne, Rudy Vallee, and Kate Smith. They were being spoon-fed their dinnertime news by such big-name commentators as Gabriel Heatter, Elmer Davis, Lowell Thomas, and Fulton Lewis, Junior. And on Sunday evenings millions would drop everything to listen to the urgent trivia of Walter Winchell, famous columnist for the Hearst newspapers, who achieved one of the highest-rated programs in radio history. Winchell made everything he said urgent by his energy and rapid-fire delivery. Throughout his broadcast he wore a hat pushed back on his head—the trademark of a working reporter—and he maintained an excitement that began with his opening: "Good evening, Mr. and Mrs. North and South America and all the ships at sea—let's go to press!" An item about a Hollywood starlet being seen with "so and so" would be given the same feverish tone as if he were reporting a declaration of war. Occasionally he had legitimate news scoops, but his hot flashes were largely gossip about political and show business personalities, with periodic plugs for his friend J. Edgar Hoover, and digs at "Commies" and "pinkos" as the Cold War grew hotter.

He was an open advocate of "tooting your own horn"—which he did loud and often—and frequently bragged about his power to make or break entertainers and to destroy his enemies.

Anyone who commands so many millions of listeners is powerful enough to influence the news as well as report it—which Winchell often did by the sheer force of his biases. Occasionally he seemed to do it deliberately, by using his vast audience to manipulate the stock market. He'd hint that a certain stock was due for a rise. Enough listeners would rush to buy it the next day to create the rise that he had predicted. Once he mentioned the prospects of a seventy-five cent oil stock—the next morning it was quickly run up several dollars. He was never charged with using this power for his own aggrandizement. Rather it seemed more an ego thing—a childish attempt to prove to himself (or to someone from his nursery days) how really powerful he had become. "Hey, look at me! I can make the stock market go up or down!" The Securities and Exchange Commission finally cracked down and spoiled his fun.

At times Winchell wielded his power on the side of the angels. This Lower East Side boy and former vaudeville hoofer founded, and raised millions of dollars for The Damon Runyon Cancer Fund.

Nineteen forty-six was also the year Norman Corwin won the Wendell Willkie-Freedom House One World Award for promoting the concept of Global Unity. On June 15 he left to collect his prize—a trip around the world, to report on what people of other countries were thinking, hoping, and planning, now that the war had ended. I had the utterly irrational feeling that I should have been taken along. After all we had been a successful combination in England, hadn't we? But my labored logic did not prevail and this time Corwin took with him only a CBS engineer—a practical companion who knew how to operate one of those new-fangled wire recorders.

Things were rather slow for me during the summer and autumn of 1946. It took a little while to let people know I was back in town and available, although I did pick up

odd jobs on *The Thin Man, Philo Vance, Mr. District At-*
torney, Inner Sanctum, Ellery Queen, Casey, Crime Pho-
tographer, Bulldog Drummond, The Second Mrs. Burton,
and *Mr. Keen, Tracer of Lost Persons.* I informed the
Hummerts I had returned, and they kept their promise to
have my role written back into *Lorenzo Jones and His Wife*
Belle. However, story lines were written well in advance,
and I had to wait several months before being called.

Meanwhile, I worked on the play I had begun on the
ship and volunteered some spare time to the Stage Door
Canteen, a recreational facility for servicemen that had
been set up in Times Square by the American Theater
Wing (an organization that had mobilized the entertainment world behind the war effort). It had established Can-
teens throughout the country, but New York City's was the
most glamorous. It was staffed by actors and actresses—bit
players and stars—who volunteered as hosts and hostesses,
waiters and waitresses. They even did the dirty work in
the kitchen. Although I never put it on my resumé, I'm
fond of bragging that I once worked with the great stage
actor, Alfred Lunt. I washed. He dried.

Fulfilling myself in the theater was still my ultimate
goal. But prospects were bleak, and radio work was an extremely painless way of surviving while awaiting that big
break on Broadway.

I began calling myself Joe instead of Joseph Julian in
the credits, on the theory that scripts frequently had characters named Joe (especially stories about servicemen) and
casting directors would just naturally think of me. I can't
prove it, but from then on it seemed as though I played a
lot of guys named Joe.

I was happy to be back with *Lorenzo Jones and His*

Wife Belle: This was one of the most delightful radio shows on the air—a jewel among the soaps, and my role ran for six years, on an average of three times a week. It was written by Theodore and Mathilde Ferro, a husband and wife team. Highly literate, it had great charm and humor. Lorenzo, brilliantly played by Karl Swenson, was a would-be inventor; I played Sandy, his admiring neighbor. Lorenzo would invent things that were almost ridiculous, but not quite. Such as the three-spout teapot, for strong, weak and medium tea. And an anti-speeding device hooked up to the radio in his car. When going over the speed limit, a tough voice would come through the loudspeaker, snarling, "Take it easy, bud!"

The show was eventually destroyed by its producers. It was the one soap opera the Hummerts didn't fabricate in their factory, nor had they insisted the writers conform to their formula. Perhaps it was their way of "atoning" for the others. Or, maybe they were just very fond of it themselves. In any case, after about ten years, when the rating slipped, they decided to broaden the base of its appeal. All the charm and distinction went out of it as they introduced their favorite ingredients—melodramatic plot lines, a murder mystery, and an Englishman for snob appeal. Alas.

I also picked up another running part in *Big Sister*, playing a role completely different from the Michael West I had originated six years before. Generally, a couple of years was considered time enough for an actor to be "forgotten" and reintroduced into the same show as a fresh character.

In 1947 I won the starring role in a new weekly show on NBC—*Call the Police*—that replaced *Amos 'n' Andy* for the summer. In it I played a police commissioner of a different stripe—a college graduate grounded in modern anti-crime methods.

The police had long been maligned in air dramas as being stupid, uneducated, and cruel, and this was an attempt to put them in a better light.

A feature of the series was an award of $100 to a "Policeman of the Week" who had performed an outstanding service beyond the call of duty.

The show had a little side dividend. The National Police Magazine published on its cover a picture of me presenting a check to a police officer. I always kept that issue in the glove compartment of my car. It got me out of two speeding tickets.

Apropos the police—one evening I picked up a copy of the New York *Mirror* and got a chill. The entire front page of the tabloid was a close-up photograph of a man's swollen and bloodied face. The caption said that he had resisted arrest on a murder charge. He had been beaten so badly identification was nearly impossible, but there was something about the crinkly corners of his swollen eyes that made me turn to the story on the inside page. It was Tom Ashwell.

He had been arrested by Florida police for murdering two young girls. From their photographs they looked like the working class girls, the "spirited little sparrow types," with whom we had double-dated. He had represented himself as a movie talent scout and was presumably driving the girls to a nearby town to have pictures made. He turned off on a side road to the woods, where he stopped, tied each girl to a tree, and, after raping them, bashed their heads in with a hammer.

Ashwell was tried and convicted, and several months later he was executed in the electric chair by the State of Florida. I thought back fifteen years, remembering his cold-blooded plan for success. Cold-blooded, yes. Success, no.

The reverberations of that horror stayed with me a long time. I usually try to distill something positive out of the shocks of my life. I don't know what I got out of that, except, perhaps, a little more respect for my intuition.

In early 1948 I won an audition for one of the two leads in another crime show, *Hearthstone of the Death Squad,* a weekly, prime-time evening series on CBS. The job lasted five years. It was, undoubtedly, one of the worst shows on the air, yet had one of the highest ratings. I'm too patriotic to draw conclusions. Hearthstone, played by English actor Alfred Shirley, was a New York cop; I was Sam, his assistant. No one ever raised the question of why a New York cop would have a broad English accent. But if they had, the answer would have been that the producers, Frank and Anne Hummert, had a theory about snob appeal. Most of their other programs also contained at least one character who was upper class, such as *Our Gal Sunday* (*Organ music*): Can a miner's daughter find happiness with England's richest Lord?

Between the Hummerts' "snobs" and radio's occasional productions of Shakespeare and other classics, there was a fairly active demand for good English speech, and there were enough English actors living in New York to supply it.

One, Harry Cliff-Cooper, who had played the voice of God in a biblical drama, was out of town when the show was repeated. He was replaced by Jay Jostyn (star of *Mr. District Attorney*), an actor with a distinctly American flavor to his speech. When a fellow actor sympathized with Cliff-Cooper for having lost the role, he replied with typical British fortitude, "Well, in this business we must take the bad with the good." And then added, quite sincerely, "But, dear boy, one does rather think of God as an Englishman, doesn't one?"

I acquired another regular weekly show, the radio version of Rex Stout's Nero Wolfe stories, first heard over ABC in 1943. For four years I played Archie, the famous fat orchid fancier's tough assistant. Santos Ortega, one of radio's busiest actors, played Nero Wolfe in a very fine, fat voice. The producer was the fabulous Himan Brown. Why fabulous? Ask anyone who knows him.

Hi was one of radio's pioneer producers, and had made a million dollars by the time he was twenty-four. When still little more than a kid, he zeroed in on what the average listener liked, and originated such radio shows as, *Marie, the Little French Princess* (one of the first soap operas); *Green Valley, U.S.A.; The Thin Man; The Gumps* (written by Irwin Shaw); *Joyce Jordan, Girl Interne; Hilda Hope, M.D.; Little Italy; Inner Sanctum; Grand Central Station; City Desk; The Affairs of Peter Salem; Flash Gordon; Bulldog Drummond; Dick Tracy;* and *Terry and the Pirates,* to mention only a few.

These were all ongoing shows, and Hi was always up to his ears in authors and actors, each daytime serial requiring five scripts, and evening shows a complete new story, every week.

The Frank and Anne Hummert factory may have turned

out a larger number of shows, but Hi Brown was a one-man operation. He produced, cast, and directed all of his shows himself. He never even had an office. He'd make his phone calls from home, or use a phone at one of the studios. He had shrewd understanding of script values and an outsize charm that seduced performers to work for him for less than they would for anyone else. But he also gave them a continuity of work on his other shows, made less demands on their time, and created a more pleasant working atmosphere. It was fun working for him.

He usually hired only the best actors, who could deliver quickly, thus saving on rehearsal pay and studio costs. On most half-hour shows he'd have only an hour and a half of rehearsal. Other directors used up to four hours.

During the first read-through for timing, Hi would sit with stopwatch in one hand, pencil in the other, slashing out lines if the script were long. And it was long more often than short (it being easier to cut than to pad). When the actors finished he'd give them the cuts to write into their scripts. There would be some rehearsal of sound effects, and usually barely enough time left over for one run-through of the complete show on mike, just before going on the air.

Most of his directions were of a technical nature. He rarely gave "performance" notes. He expected his actors to know their craft. That's why he hired them. And, in the vast majority of the cases, his system worked well.

Hi Brown was radio's champion corner cutter. I think it was programmed into his genes. And that was one major reason for his success. All those corners added up, and he was usually able to sell a program at a lower price than his competitors.

11. The Eclipse

Nineteen forty-eight and nineteen forty-nine were probably the busiest years of my radio acting career. To
the end of the decade I was happily hopping from one
show to another, hiring a stand-in to rehearse for me here
while I did a show there, frequently turning jobs down for
lack of time. Between my regular, running roles, I worked
on the myriad shows, a few of which I take from the yel-
lowed pages of my old account book:

Casey, Crime Photographer
The Falcon
The Shadow
Believe It or Not
Front Page Dramas
School of the Air
Counterspy
Boston Blackie
Inner Sanctum
Mysterious Traveler
Nora Drake
Greatest Story Ever Told

General Electric Theatre
Mr. Chameleon
Mr. Keen
Wendy Warren and the News
Up for Parole
Road of Life
Two Thousand Plus
Backstage Wife
David Amity
Voice of America drama
Front Page Farrell
Joyce Jordan, Girl Interne
Café Istanbul
Against the Storm
Aunt Jenny's True Life Stories
Hilltop House
Gasoline Alley
Frank Merriwell
Hobby Lobby
Superman
Young Doctor Malone
Broadway is My Beat
Second Mrs. Burton
Portia Faces Life
When a Girl Marries
Perry Mason
We, the Living
The Goldbergs
Gene Autry Show
Hollywood Love Story
The Ramparts We Watch
Time Bomb

My curve of activity and income rose steadily through 1947, '48 and '49. Then, in 1950, it turned down and rapidly declined until, in 1953, I earned a mere $1630.

How was it possible for such a busy actor to lose his

marketability so quickly? The answer was: a U.S. Senator, Joe McCarthy. Exploiting the Cold War between the United States and Russia, McCarthy smeared, with a wide red brush, everyone who stood in his way, including President Eisenhower and the United States Army. Any political liberal, or anyone vaguely to the left of right, might suddenly be labeled a Communist or a fellow traveler by the Senator. Left became a dirty word. A joke of the time: "I have no left foot. Only a right foot number two." But it was not very funny.

The Watergate hearings were a tea party compared to the uproar on the televised hearings of the Senate Sub-Committee on Un-American Activities, presided over by Joe McCarthy. His brutal brow-beating of witnesses and dramatic denunciations of individuals created a climate of fear throughout the country. The mighty trembled, and did nothing, as McCarthy laid waste reputations, careers, and lives. Playing on the fear of war with Russia, McCarthy assumed a heroic posture as he "exposed" more and more "subversives" at home. The forces of ignorance and Fascism rallied to him and became his main support.

The Senate subcommittee generated outside pressure groups, and blacklisting organizations developed all over the country.

After intimidating Hollywood into firing and not hiring some of its most creative talents, the witch hunters turned their blacklisting passion to radio and television. These media were even more vulnerable. Products and profits were more directly associated with individual performers, and a threat of boycott quickly scared sponsors into dropping those who had a finger pointed at them, whether the

accusations were true or not. They reasoned, "Why risk
the loss of customers when there are plenty of 'safe' actors
around?"

Actors are notoriously generous in donating their time
and talent to causes. When asked, they find it difficult to
say no. Frequently they agree to perform at functions without probing deeply into the sponsorship. Many lost their
livelihood for that reason alone. Also, Russia had been our
ally during the war, and there were still many Russian-
American friendship organizations. Prior to the Cold War,
it had been possible to talk to professional colleagues who
were Communists, or Communist sympathizers, although
you might have disagreed with their politics. But the
number of actual revolutionaries was small, and the threat
of their subverting the broadcast industry nil.

The atmosphere around the studios became heavy with
fear, suspicion, and hate. Some board members of our own
union, The American Federation of Television and Radio
Artists, helped form a pressure group, Aware, Inc., to force
the banning of all Communists and sympathizers (by their
definition) from the airwaves. At union meetings they
openly advocated blacklisting and split the union wide
open. Those who voted against it were carefully noted,
and things happened to them. Like being fired. Or not
being hired.

There was a close liaison between Aware, Inc. and the
House Committee on Un-American Activities in Washington, and Lawrence Johnson, the owner of several supermarkets in Syracuse, New York. The first two supplied
the names; Johnson was the enforcer. Johnson's clout
stemmed from the fact that he owned six supermarkets on

whose shelves stood the majority of products advertised on radio and TV. When he was fed a name to do a job on, he'd shoot off a telegram to the sponsor asking: DO YOU WANT STALIN'S LITTLE CREATURES CRAWLING ALL OVER YOUR PRODUCTS?, coupled with a threat to remove said product from the shelves of all six of his stores if the sponsor didn't fire the tainted actor. That was a powerful persuader, pardner. The "Grocer from Syracuse," as he became known, would follow up with personal visits to Madison Avenue, to persuade the advertising agencies to do his bidding. He usually got results. The actor never knew what had hit him.

I was appalled as more and more of my friends faded from the scene. I wasn't worried for myself. Whatever sympathy I had for the poor and downtrodden in Russia, I had very early been opposed to the brutal dictatorship of Stalin and I had always been forthright in my opinion that the light that went into the bottom of the Russian revolution was no longer shed from the top. Why would anyone blacklist me?

I was naïve. On June 22, 1950, I was shocked out of my complacency by the publication of *Red Channels: The Report of Communist Influence in Radio and Television,* a paperbound volume listing 151 actors, directors, producers, writers, announcers, musicians, and commentators, and their associations with organizations accused of furthering the Communist cause. My name was among them.

The cover of the book had a huge, bloody, red hand clutching a microphone, and despite an attempt at a legal disclaimer by burying in the fine print of the introduction—"In screening personnel, every safeguard must be used to protect innocents and genuine liberals from being unjustly labeled"—the implication was clear that everyone in that book was subversive and should be kept off the air.

Vincent Hartnett, a former production assistant on the radio show, *Gangbusters,* claimed credit for conceiving, compiling, and writing the introduction to the book, but it was given instant status by Ed Sullivan, the influential columnist of the New York *Daily News,* who wrote:

> With television going into its third big year, come this Fall, the entire industry is becoming increasingly aware of the necessity to plug all Commie propaganda loopholes.
>
> Network and station heads, with a tremendous financial stake, want no part of Commies or pinkos.
>
> Sponsors, sensitive in the extreme to blacklisting, want no part of Commies or their sympathizers.
>
> Advertising agencies, held responsible by sponsors for correct exercise of discretion in programming, want no controversy of any kind.
>
> For that reason, *Red Channels'* listing of performers, who, innocently or maliciously, are affiliated with Commie-front organizations, will be a reference book in preparing any program.

So it came to pass. Copies of *Red Channels* were sent to all radio and television stations, advertising agencies, and casting directors. Now, at last, there was an "authoritative" blacklist that could be kept handy in a desk drawer. And it wreaked havoc on the lives of those listed.

My listing was minuscule compared to most of the others in the book, some of which amounted to forty-one entries. This is the way my name appeared, connecting me with two allegedly subversive organizations, and the sources of this information:

JOE JULIAN
Actor—Radio.   Reported as:
Artists' Front to   Speaker. Meeting
Win the War   10/16/42. House Un-Am.
                                 Act. Com., Appendix 9,
                                 p. 575.
National Council of   Attended meeting to abolish
the Arts, Sciences   House Un-American Activities
and Professions.   Committee, Hotel Commodore,
                                 NYC, 1/9/49
                                 NY Journal-American
                                 12/30/48.50

The facts: When I returned from London in 1942 I was invited to read in Carnegie Hall a poem about artists who died fighting Fascism. The meeting, organized by a committee called Artists' Front to Win the War, was to further sentiment for the opening of a second front in Europe, which was being called for by President Roosevelt and most U.S. military leaders. A second front was also advocated by a number of prominent anti-Communists, such as author Louis Bromfield, Lord Beaverbrook, and Dorothy Thompson. Some of the speakers were Orson Welles, Charlie Chaplin, Mary Margaret McBride—a wide spectrum of political coloration. The list of sponsors read like a Who's Who of the American Theater.

This was my one and only connection with that committee, which eight years later was termed subversive by some small California committee of state legislators.

My other "crime" was having attended a public rally on January 9, 1949 at the Hotel Commodore in New York, called by the National Committee of Arts, Sciences and Professions, to abolish the House Un-American Activities Committee. This widely-advertised rally featured Burt

Lancaster as the main speaker. I indeed attended, since I was personally sympathetic to the purpose of the meeting, namely, to protest censorship and the disgraceful conduct of the Chairman of the House Un-American Activities Committee, Parnell Thomas, who was later sent to prison.

Nevertheless, those two citations in *Red Channels* cost me my livelihood for over three years.

This was an ugly period in American life and in mine, and I find it difficult to write about. My urge is to skip over it. Others, better qualified, have documented the history and scope of blacklisting in the broadcast industry. But I do feel a responsibility as a victim to record some of what I went through. A whole new generation hardly knows that such a thing ever happened. But the fact is it could easily happen again if we relax our vigilance in defending our freedoms. Control of broadcasting is one of the first major objectives of those who would take them away.

My initial reaction to the publication of *Red Channels* was anger and indignation—not panic or fear of economic loss. At that time I had no concept of what was to follow. I was furious at being misrepresented, at being labeled a subversive. And so, when I heard that a number of "listees" were meeting in the office of Attorney Arthur Garfield Hays to plan legal action, I made it my business to be there.

Hays, a wrinkled, leathery man in his eighties, was a famous civil libertarian, who, along with Clarence Darrow, had been one of the defense lawyers in the renowned Scopes "Monkey Trial."

There were eight or nine performers at the meeting, and the majority urged Hays to represent them in a mass libel suit. He told them he was outraged by the book and offered to represent everyone individually on a contingency basis, but not as a group—and only if they could convince him that they had in fact been libeled.

Only four actors agreed to that: Ralph Bell, Pert Kelton, Selena Royal, and me, confirming Hays' feeling (as he later told me) that the others wanted the group action in order to use us to mask their membership or former membership in the Communist Party.

I had a couple of private meetings with Hays, during which he questioned me closely, especially about my political beliefs. Convinced that I had been libeled, in December 1950 he filed suit on my behalf against the American Business Consultants, publishers of *Red Channels,* for $150,000 in damages. It was four years before the case reached the courtroom—four wretched years of declining work, income, and morale.

Things didn't happen abruptly: everyone in the book wasn't fired the day after publication. Except in a few prominent cases, those who were contracted were kept on until their contracts expired. As for the work-a-day actor, he gradually began getting fewer calls. Not many producers and directors were sympathetic to blacklisting, but as the heat was increasingly poured on by the "Grocer from Syracuse," his confederates within the union, and others, *Red Channels* became more and more, as Ed Sullivan predicted, "a reference book in preparing any programs."

There were a few courageous employers—even sponsors, who bucked the tide, but the vast majority eventually succumbed to the pressures. A number of directors told me in confidence, "I want to use you, Joe, but it would cost me my job."

Most weren't that frank. They made excuses, or avoided speaking to me altogether. And that was the insidious part—the victims rarely knew for sure why they were no longer called. And that sparked the old syndrome: "It was my fault. I've been giving lousy performances. I've lost my talent, etc." If the odds were ninety-nine to one that it was because of *Red Channels*, actors would dwell on the one percent possibility that it was their own fault. The black-list played hell with our fragile egos. Actors need to act. The loss of function was worse than loss of income. It led to a terrible erosion of faith in ourselves, both as artists and as productive members of society.

I spent a great deal of my time just hanging around the studio lobbies racking my brains for a way to earn money. My bank account was dwindling fast. I still had one regular evening show each week, *Hearthstone of the Death Squad*, for which I was paid $125, but it wasn't nearly enough to meet my obligations. The show had been on several years, and I had been promised a twenty-five dollar raise, which seemed to have been forgotten. I decided to call on the producer's business manager. He greeted me politely, asked me to sit down, and before I could explain my mission, opened his middle desk drawer, and took out a copy of *Red Channels*.

"Mr. Julian, I see your name listed in this book," he said, his raised eyebrows inviting an explanation. His strategy was clear. He knew why I was there. Actors usually came to discuss money matters, and he was cutting the ground from under me.

He listened attentively while I explained at length why I should not have been listed. Then I reminded him of the promised raise. He slipped the book back in the drawer. I don't recall his exact words, but the raise was refused. And loud and clear between the lines I heard, "Now get the hell out of here and be glad you still have a job!"

I didn't much longer. Some months later that show went off the air. Now I was really in the straits of dire. I seriously thought of going back to selling shoes on Forty-second Street. Every day I pored over want ads, stupidly hoping to find a good job for which no experience was necessary. I wanted to fight out of the situation with all my strength, but I no longer knew how, or in what direction to move. I felt helpless.

I asked myself who was the most influential person I knew in broadcasting? I remembered that the president of CBS, William Paley, had sent for me when I returned from London. I figured I couldn't do better than going to the top. I wrote him a letter:

Dear Mr. Paley,

Since I've been in radio I have worked on literally thousands of CBS broadcasts. You may remember me as the "American" in your *American in England* series during the war.

At the present time I am barred from working on CBS radio or television shows by virtue of my listing in *Red Channels*. This I have learned from several sources. I am sure you are unaware of the injustice being done me.

The subversion implied by the listing of my name in *Red Channels* is grossly libelous and I have entered a libel suit against the publishers for $150,000 damages. I have never been a member of any organization listed as subversive by the Attorney General, and have signed the CBS oath to that effect. Politically, I am and always have been equally opposed to totalitarianism of the left or the right, and any form of government that devalues the basic rights of the individual.

I am writing to you, Mr. Paley, because I am being deprived

of my livelihood. I realize you are too busy to deal with all the cases of individual actors who are caught in the squeeze of this monstrous problem of our times, but I would be grateful if you would advise me what further steps I can take in order to resume working for CBS.

Sincerely,
Joseph Julian

I received a brief reply. Paley stated he had turned my letter over to Dan O'Shea, a CBS Vice President, and suggested I contact him.

O'Shea, a former Hollywood executive, was Chief Security Officer at CBS and had developed a rigorous screening system. I had heard that a number of blacklist victims had gone to him, confessed their sins, and received absolution—and help in restoring their careers.

I went to see Mr. O'Shea. Having nothing to confess, I explained my listing in *Red Channels* and how desperate my work situation was.

A large, avuncular man, he seemed to listen sympathetically as he moved about his well-appointed office smoking a large cigar. When I finished he told me that he believed everything I had said, but asked why I had only stressed what I had *not* done. What active steps had I ever taken to *fight* Communism? he wanted to know. I told him I was not a political activist, that most of my contribution was in argumentation. He said that that wasn't enough. In order to help me, he would have to have more to go on. He suggested I could do myself a lot of good by attending some American Legion rallies or joining General Lucius Clay's Crusade for Freedom. And he strongly implied that things would be much better for me if I dropped my lawsuit.

Shortly after that, the Crusade for Freedom had a rally in Times Square. I volunteered to make a pitch over a loudspeaker for cash contributions to further the work of the Crusade in broadcasting to people behind the Iron Curtain.

I felt queasy doing it, and after three or four minutes stopped. My conscience would not allow me to go on, in view of my aversion to the hard-core sponsorship of the Crusade. The extreme right was just as unpalatable to me as the extreme left.

Technically, I had taken a step toward clearance. But I couldn't bring myself to follow through on O'Shea's suggestions. And at this point it was unthinkable that I drop my lawsuit. So I continued to be unemployed.

My only real hope now was vindication in court. But it had been two years since I filed suit! I wrote a letter to Arthur Garfield Hays, asking whether my case couldn't be speeded up because of economic hardship:

> . . . things have reached the desperate stage with me. I am heavily in debt. I have cashed in my insurance policy to pay my rent and grocery bills. I can no longer earn a living in my profession. By the way, a former CBS director told me yesterday that he would be glad to testify when my case comes to trial, that he wanted me for a part and was ordered not to call me because my name is in the book. I have accumulated quite a list of people who have given me such information. . . .

But Hays could do nothing. The court calendars were hopelessly clogged.

During this period I often fought off frightening fantasies of pushing certain pro-blacklisting union officials under a subway train. I was shocked to find myself speculating on how many broken lives it might redeem, and whether I could ever really bring myself to do such a thing. It was one of those questions pacifists tortured one another with: "Could you personally kill Hitler if you knew it would save millions of lives?"

During those desperate years of unemployment and frustration for so many talented people—a number of whom committed suicide—I fortunately managed to survive by discovering a market for my talent that the "Grocer from Syracuse" didn't seem to know or care about: narrating industrial, institutional, and training films. Most of it was sixteen-millimeter material that had no general public exposure, and therefore was not subject to the same blacklisting pressures. It was painful, but I swallowed whatever pride I had accumulated and went from company to company soliciting auditions. Occasionally I landed a job. I soon discovered that most of these filmmakers had been using pontificating radio announcers as narrators, and were delighted to find their films enhanced by the feeling of simple truth that a narrator with an acting background could bring to his reading. These jobs just barely kept my nostrils above water.

Ironically, during this period when radio stations and advertising agencies wouldn't hire me because of my "subversive" associations, one of these film companies (MPO Films) engaged me to act the on-camera role of a five-star general in a secret film being made only for the eyes of a special U.S. congressional committee, about how our Strategic Air Command would function in case of an enemy attack. We shot the film in the super-secret headquarters control room of the Strategic Air Command, deep in the bowels of the earth at Omaha, Nebraska, where guards were posted every fifty yards and permission to enter was given only to those who had been thoroughly investigated and approved by the FBI. That, I suppose, is as eloquent a comment as can be made on the blacklisting insanity that prevailed in the name of national defense.

During the shooting of this film, I went to the men's room one day, wearing my general's uniform. Standing next to me was an Air Force colonel (a real one). He did a double-take as he noticed my five stars, and became utterly uncoordinated. Torn between lifting his occupied right hand in a salute or withdrawing and zipping up first, he made several false starts in both directions before saluting. It was a disaster. I returned his salute. I didn't dare risk his wrath by telling him who I really was.

Early in 1954 Hays informed me that my case was on the calendar. He said we had a few more weeks to prepare, and instructed me to line up witnesses who would testify they didn't employ me only because my name was in *Red Channels.*

Although I had faced juries in hundreds of radio dramas, this was my first real-life courtroom adventure, and my eagerness was tinged with apprehension. I had been told New York State libel laws were notoriously complex; that both damages and malice had to be proven; that findings for the plaintiff were rare; that libel is one lawsuit where the plaintiff is on the defensive all the time, and that the defendants will raise whatever extraneous issues they can to further blacken the character and credibility of the plaintiff: me.

Too, the mere prospect of appearing in court can make one feel a smidgen of culpability. Since there are no abso-

lutes in this world, how can we be sure we are ever completely innocent? The very prospect of being judged
evokes a Kafkaesque echo of infantile or prenatal or prehis-
toric guilt. But I banished most of these negative feelings
with a determination to fight as hard as I could; energetically I began my search for witnesses.

But they weren't to be had for the asking. Nor for the
pleading, arguing, or cajoling. By now blacklists had pro-
liferated, and merely being seen in the company of a *Red
Channels* listee was enough to land you on somebody's
list. The intimidation of the industry was so thorough that
even those who had promised to testify changed their
minds. The starch went out of even the brave ones. I
couldn't really blame them. They, too, had families to support. But without evidence or testimony that I had been
deprived of work by my listing in *Red Channels*, I had no
case. It was terribly disheartening. For the previous four
years the promise of legal salvation had kept me going. It
had been my only hope. And now that was dimming.

Still, I daily haunted the hangouts of radio actors, writers,
and directors—the third floor lobby at NBC and Colbee's
Restaurant in the old CBS building—searching out every
crumb of support.

There was plenty of moral support, but nothing to support my morale; much sympathy but not a single commitment. No one dared stick his neck out.

But persistence finally paid off. Someone did dare. He
was having a quick noontime bolster at Colbee's bar as I
approached and said, "Ed, I'm suing *Red Channels* for
libel. Will you be a witness for me?" Without the slightest
hesitation, without asking a single question, without speculating for a fraction of a second about how an appear-

ance on my behalf might compromise his position at CBS, he replied, "Tell me when and where, Joe." That's the kind of a man Edward R. Murrow was.

It gave my spirit an enormous lift. I knew that just his presence in court on my behalf would count heavily. He also promised to bring along another character witness, Charles Collingwood, the well-known CBS foreign correspondent, whom I had met in London. Things were looking up. I was beginning to regain confidence.

I had a two-hour "trailer" of the trial, at a pre-trial examination called by the defendants, mainly as a fishing expedition. The biggest fish they caught was an acknowledgment by me that I had at home a few ancient *Theatre Arts Monthly* magazines, which were alleged to have been published by some Communist front organization.

They also used the occasion (off the record) to try to convince me to drop my suit. I refused. They strongly implied that they would see I got work, and cited a well-known Broadway and Hollywood actor, listed in *Red Channels,* who had threatened to sue but was persuaded to talk it over. He dropped the suit and found himself again in demand.

I couldn't do it. The momentum was too great. Ed Murrow and the angels were on my side, and I was going to win. Besides I had a growing awareness of the larger importance of my suit. Other victims had a stake in my fight. A solid verdict would be a smashing blow to the entire structure of blacklisting. I vigorously went after more witnesses.

I remembered that Marjorie Morrow, an agent and a dear lady, told me she had submitted me a number of times to the *Philip Morris Playhouse,* always with the same "Can't-use-him-he's-in-*Red Channels*" response. Asked if she would so testify in court, she said no, she was already in trouble just for having submitted my name. I told her I could subpoena and force her to testify under oath. Almost in tears, she asked me not to. Hers was a small agency, and it would ruin her. "Promise me you won't," she begged. I promised.

But it gave me another idea. The director of the *Philip Morris Playhouse*, Charles Martin, was a bright, erratic, liberal, temperamental young writer-director, who had made it to the top in radio by using a little properly channeled imagination. I wondered if he might be just courageous or neurotic enough to agree to testify where others wouldn't. It was worth a try.

I phoned Hays. First I told him how I had threatened Marge Morrow with a subpoena and why we couldn't go through with it. He said he rarely forced a witness to court anyway, because he liked to be sure of what they were going to say.

I told him about Martin and suggested we call on him. I figured it would be easier for Hays to get an appointment than for me, and that a man famous for swaying juries would be much more apt to persuade Martin to testify.

We met in Martin's apartment a few days later, where for an hour he warded off our pleas, even though he had strong feelings against the blacklist. He also had a high-salaried job and didn't want to lose it.

I argued that his employer wouldn't hold him responsible if he were "forced" to appear and tell the truth under oath. And I impressed him with the fact that Ed Murrow was going to be a witness for me.

Hays too stressed the Murrow name, playing on Martin's

ego and idealism. You could see Martin growing larger and sitting straighter as Hays eloquently wove a hero's mantle around him. He told him this was a great opportunity to bust the blacklisting business wide open; that he, Charles Martin, could help turn the tide the way Murrow's famous broadcast documenting Joe McCarthy's villainy helped to generally turn the country away from McCarthyism. Martin succumbed. Not weakly, but embracing the cause wholeheartedly. Now I had my first and only witness to support a claim of damages.

Character witnesses were easier to acquire. In addition to Murrow and Collingwood, Robert Saudek, producer of the Ford Foundation's *Omnibus* program—the man who a decade earlier had produced my "Dover Diary"—and writer Morton Wishengrad agreed to testify.*

Finally, I was notified by Mr. Hays that my case would be called for trial on February 26, 1954.

* Wishengrad, who died a number of years ago, was in my opinion the only writer other than Corwin who created a body of radio literature that deserves a perennial life. And many of the little stories he wrote have been and are still being repeated on NBC's Sunday *Eternal Light* program. Written with biblical simplicity, and sponsored by the Jewish Theological Seminary, they were not religious in the narrow sense. And although he drew on his vast knowledge of ancient Jewish lore, his stories, informed by his own sweet humor and fineness of spirit, had an ecumenical appeal.

12. The Trial

As we entered the courtroom that first day Hays was optimistic. Truth was on our side, we now had some good witnesses and good evidence—and we were to plead before Justice Abraham Geller, who had a reputation as a fair-minded liberal.

But there was an immediate setback: as the jury selection began, the attorneys for the defendants produced a list of some 200 organizations, and asked the judge for permission to disqualify any juror who ever had the remotest connection with any of them. Judge Geller asked to see the list. After studying it a few moments he said, "I see you have here the American Civil Liberties Union. Why, I myself used to be a dues-paying member of that organization."

Whereupon Ed Wallace, the chief defense lawyer, said, "Therefore, your Honor, we ask you to disqualify yourself from sitting on this case."

And Judge Geller complied.

I was shocked, even though Hays explained to me that it

was customary in a civil suit for a judge to disqualify him-self if either party requests it.

It was three months before the case was called again, this time before Judge Irving Saypol. I have no knowledge of how the assignment was made. I have no evidence that it was more than a coincidence. But it was mighty strange that, among other things, Saypol just happened to have been the U.S. Attorney who prosecuted Julius and Ethel Rosenberg and helped send them to the electric chair.

At our first appearance in his court, on May 17, 1954, Judge Saypol said, "Mr. Hays, before we proceed, I would like to remind you that you and I have had many disagree-ments in the past. I would also like to inform you that Mr. Wallace, counsel for the defendants, used to be my execu-tive assistant. In view of that I would like to know if your client would feel uneasy if I tried this case?"

Ah! Now our side had a break. We conferred a fast two seconds, then Hays said, "Yes, your Honor, we would like you to disqualify yourself."

Saypol said he would give his answer after lunch, and declared a recess.

When the court reconvened he said he had thought it over and had decided that he would be remiss in his duty if he stepped down. He ordered the case to proceed.

It was incredible. Not only his flouting custom, but the way he had set it up, asking us, and then. . . .

I asked Hays if we had no legal recourse. He said the best strategy was not to make an issue of it. That would put the burden on Saypol to bend over backward to be fair. But it didn't work that way. I'm no expert in the fine points of legal contention, but I know hostility when I feel it. And it was there throughout the five days we presented

our case. Perhaps some of it was the ingrained aggres-
siveness of the prosecutor Saypol had once been and to
which he frequently reverted as he leaned over and ham-
mered questions at my witnesses from the bench. The
transcript of the trial shows the judge asking my witnesses
almost as many questions as the defense counsel did. Most
of the time he gave the impression he was developing the
defendants' case for them.

His attitude toward Hays, who behaved with meticulous
decorum, was reflected in this little colloquy when he denied one of his objections:

HAYS: Then your Honor denies me the right to state the rea-
sons for my objections?
SAYPOL: No. It is immaterial.
HAYS: I want to state my reasons.
SAYPOL: I don't need them. If I want I will ask for them.
HAYS: I understand that, but I want to make it perfectly clear
on the record that your Honor denies me the right to state the
reasons for my objection.
SAYPOL: I believe you have adequately stated them.

Spoken, it sounded even more arrogant. And that was
the general tone of the proceedings.

I was sworn as the first witness in my own behalf. Hays
had put me at ease by assuring me that the best witness
was a truthful one, and that I had no reason to be anything
but.

He led me through my early background, with questions
calculated to elicit answers that would touch the jurors'
emotions, such as the fact that my mother had died when I
was an infant and my father when I was twelve; that I
lived with an aunt and uncle for a time, then in an orphan-
age; that I later boarded in a home for working boys, sold

newspapers, worked in a candy store and a shoe factory; became interested in amateur theatricals; started professionally as an extra for a dollar a night with a stock company that came to town.

Hays was so sympathetic when he dwelt on my orphanhood that it embarrassed me. And, in stressing how I had overcome my deprived childhood and gone on to professional achievements, he must have harvested more sympathy from the jury. "Get 'em emotionally from the start," seemed the strategy of this famous trial lawyer.

He traced my career up to and a few years beyond the publication of *Red Channels* when my income fell to almost nothing. I produced verifying tax records showing that during the first four months of the then current year, 1954, my income was $309.

The defense tried to establish on cross-examination that my lack of employment was the result of television's impact on radio, and that I was essentially a radio actor. Over a period of several years I had compiled a list of directors who had told me of specific occasions when they had wanted me for both radio and television shows, but had not been permitted to hire me because I was in *Red Channels*. His Honor would not permit me to testify to what these directors had told me.

But the real rub came when my other important witnesses were blocked from contributing crucial testimony by defense objections that were upheld by the judge.

For instance, Davidson Taylor, director of public affairs for NBC, was only allowed to testify to my reputation as an actor. He was not allowed to give his opinion about my reputation for loyalty or veracity—which to my nonlegalistic mind seemed highly relevant in a case of libel.

Charles Collingwood was not allowed to answer Hays' question about my reputation as a man of loyalty, integrity, and as a good citizen. Nor was Ed Murrow. And when Hays asked Murrow, "Are you familiar with the customs of the television and radio business in connection with the employment of actors, so that you can tell me whether or not there is a custom in the business that men whose names are listed in *Red Channels* should not be employed?" Murrow was not permitted to respond because he himself did not specifically have to do with the hiring of actors, even though he was at that time a CBS vice-president and fully aware of the company's policy.

Charles Martin was probably my most valuable witness. He rose to the occasion splendidly. He acted it up a bit, shrugging and making shocked grimaces to the jury as the judge or defense lawyer restricted his testimony. But he persisted in his central statement that he was not permitted to hire any actor listed in *Red Channels*.

An excerpt of his direct examination by Hays:

HAYS: Mr. Martin, what is your business or profession?

MARTIN: I am a producer and director and writer occasionally of radio, television and motion pictures.

HAYS: And how long have you been in that business or profession?

MARTIN: Well, I have functioned in this capacity for more than sixteen years.

HAYS: Do you, in connection with your work, pick out persons as artists or actors?

MARTIN: I have sole jurisdiction, I would say, as to who works for our shows other than whatever blocks are put on me by the people above me. But the client has placed me in charge of casting. I think every director and producer does his own casting, largely, in this industry.

HAYS: Can you tell us some of the shows you are producing today?

MARTIN: Well, the *Philip Morris Playhouse*, radio-television. I have written for *The March of Time, Criminal Court*, I have done several films for MGM, Universal, I have done innumerable radio shows, the *Tallulah Bankhead Show*, which I wrote and directed, the *Gertrude Lawrence Show*.

SAYPOL: They can be counted, can't they? You say innumerable. I'm sure somebody can count them.

MARTIN: Forgive me, your Honor.

SAYPOL: You don't want to say how many?

MARTIN: I don't know how many, actually. But I have done a great many shows.

HAYS: Do you remember when the book *Red Channels* was published?

MARTIN: I don't remember when it was published. I remember when it was given to me.

HAYS: And about when was that?

MARTIN: A copy of *Red Channels* was given to me in the year 1950, I would say, when I returned from Hollywood, after having done some films, and had returned to radio.

HAYS: Did you ever refuse to give Joe Julian a job as an actor on any of your shows for the sole reason that his name appeared in *Red Channels?*

WALLACE: Objection.

SAYPOL: I will allow it.

MARTIN: I did refuse to give Mr. Julian employment on our shows because his name was in *Red Channels.*

HAYS: Did you regard Joe Julian as a competent, able actor?

MARTIN: Well, it's my opinion that he is a very brilliant actor.

HAYS: And what were the circumstances under which you refused to give him a job at the time you mentioned? Do you know which show it was?

MARTIN: It was the *Playhouse*, the *Philip Morris Playhouse* on TV.

HAYS: And at what salary? What salary did that part carry?

MCGRODY (defense): Objection, if your Honor pleases. This, again would be specifically on special damages.

SAYPOL: I will hear it. You may answer.

MARTIN: Well, there was a $500 part open.

HAYS: $500 for what, for one performance?

MARTIN: For one performance, of course.

HAYS: And was this a continuous job that he would get if you employed him? I mean would it be week after week?

MARTIN: I have a nucleus, more or less, like a stock company, and the good, non-name players, as we refer to them in the trade, we put into the stock company, who work more or less every week or every other week. So that this saves us, the director, a lot of trouble in going all over town and continually auditioning new actors; whereas if we get good, sturdy, reliable actors we continually use them in different roles because of their variety of talents.

HAYS: And this would have been a job that would have given Joe Julian $500 a week for about how many weeks?

WALLACE: Objection.

SAYPOL: Sustained.

HAYS: Was there more than one occasion on which you refused to give Joe Julian a job because his name was in *Red Channels*.

MCGRODY: Same objection, if your Honor please.

SAYPOL: Sustained.

HAYS: Now, did you have work for Joe Julian for a long period of time?

WALLACE: Objection.

SAYPOL: He may answer specifically, not in a general way.

MARTIN: I had several jobs for him.

SAYPOL: You have or you have had?

MARTIN: I have had.

HAYS: And you refused to hire him on all these jobs because his name was in *Red Channels?*

WALLACE: Objection.

SAYPOL: He may answer subject to a motion to strike out.

MARTIN: I was instructed—

McGRODY: Objection.

SAYPOL: Well now, do I understand that this non-hiring was on the basis of your own conclusion, your own judgment, or because somebody else told you to?

MARTIN: Somebody else told me to.

SAYPOL: I see. We will strike out all the testimony, then. You don't know anything about it.

WALLACE: I move to strike out all the testimony that has been given.

SAYPOL: Strike it out. I thought this man was the man who made the decision.

HAYS: He just didn't hire him. And he was the man charged with . . .

SAYPOL: It's hearsay. The man decided that this plaintiff was either a Communist or a dupe or an innocent on the basis either of what somebody else told him or on the basis of his construction of *Red Channels*.

HAYS: I didn't ask him about that, your Honor. I asked him whether that was the reason he wouldn't hire him.

SAYPOL: No, he says somebody else told him not to. That's hearsay. I can't allow that. Somebody may not have liked the color of Julian's tie and told him it was because his name was in *Red Channels*.

That kind of ruling against Martin's testimony was typical. Here Martin, in a hiring position and intimately acquainted with blacklisting procedure, swore under oath that he didn't employ me *only* because my name was in that book, yet this was rejected as hearsay. Even if someone else told him to do it, Martin himself blacklisted me, and it seemed to me his testimony to that effect should have been permitted.

Saypol also helped the defense by using my own witnesses against me when he asked Murrow, Collingwood, and the others: "Can you say, as a matter of knowledge, that as a direct and well-connected result of the publication of his name in this book, *Red Channels,* he has been avoided and shunned by former friends and acquaintances?" They could hardly have answered affirmatively, not knowing who my friends and acquaintances were.

Their negative answers implied, or were intended to imply, that therefore my reputation had suffered no damage. Indeed, the judge cited the presence of these distinguished men themselves in court on my behalf to buttress that inference.

Martin, in answering that question, said that he had not shunned me, but thought I had a red label. "I maintain that everybody in that book has a label attached to him," he said, "and that we—our clients—we are not interested in using the people who are in the book."

There were many moments of dramatic conflict— especially on re-cross-examination of Martin, when, like the prosecutor he had been, the Judge bore down heavily on Martin's testimony that everyone in *Red Channels* had a red label on him. In fact, during the entire presentation of my case most of the testimony favorable to me, including that of other witnesses on my behalf, was ruled inadmissible.

Each day I came to court more worried and depressed. Yet I had a gut feeling we were getting through to the jury, in spite of all the legalistic walls that were thrown up. They looked like an alert and sympathetic bunch of men and women, and I cast my hopes entirely with them on the fifth day of the trial, when our last witness stepped down and Hays said: "Plaintiff rests your Honor."

The Court recessed until the next day.

In the morning, lawyers for both sides made motions;

argued relevancy of rulings in previous cases, etc. The session ended with the defendants renewing an earlier motion to dismiss my suit at this point without going into their defense. Again Saypol promised a fateful answer after lunch.

When we reconvened he gave his decision. It took about half an hour. He read aloud parts of the Introduction to *Red Channels*, bits of testimony, and quoted lawbook cases which guided his conclusion. I listened hard, hard, trying to follow all the convolutions of his reasoning. I strained to perceive a glimpse of my fate behind his words. But the longer he spoke the less I understood. It all fudged in my mind. . . .

> . . . question arises which belongs to a class in which perplexing laws are not infrequently in reverse ratio to *Werner versus Nelson,* but the pertinent qualifying and controlling language pages six and seven where there's red smoke there's Communist fire nevertheless the favorable presumption the law permits to be inferred by eliciting from witnesses *Mencher versus Chesley* objections bound by the weight of mitigating evidence as in the case of. . . .

That's how it sounded—until he came to the final sentence, which was stunningly clear:

> Therefore Defendants' motion to dismiss at the close of plaintiff's case is granted.

It was all over. I was numb with disbelief. He wouldn't even let it go to the jury!

He gave as his reason that we had not presented a *prima-facie* case—no central question of fact for the jury to decide. This in spite of Martin's testimony that he had refused to employ me solely because my name was in that book with a bloody red hand clutching a microphone on its cover, and evidence that my income plunged drastically upon publication of *Red Channels*.

A sinking feeling of hopelessness set in, then a rising outrage. Hays put his arm around my shoulder and said, "Joe, always remember. Sometimes you win, but you never lose if your cause is just." I've tried to hang on to that thought.

If it seems arrogant for an actor to judge a judge, to question decisions of a man presumably learned in law, who carefully wrapped his rulings in precedent, let me say that, as the Devil can cite Scripture to his purpose, so a judge can, either consciously or otherwise, select only those previous rulings that support his inclination. And even they usually have some variation of circumstance.

After reading through a transcript of the trial twenty years later, Saypol's inclination was obvious. Even with the perspective of time, here in the court of my own head I still overrule his decision and find him guilty of having blatantly denied me justice.

The New York Times published a long Sunday article entitled "Case Dismissed," about Saypol's neglect of the moral issues in relation to the libel laws. *Variety* and *I. F. Stone's Weekly* ran similar pieces. My case became a minor *cause célèbre*.

Attorney Louis Nizer, who later, in a better political climate, won a similar libel suit for radio commentator John Henry Falk, told me that he felt that Hays had mishandled my case; that he was really too old and no longer sharp enough on legal points.

Ed Murrow and Charles Collingwood, and Robert Saudek of the Ford Foundation, also told me they felt frustrated at not being able to contribute more to my cause because Hays didn't ask them the right questions when they were on the witness stand. Be that as it may, the sincerity and humanity of Arthur Garfield Hays were his greatest assets, and if Saypol had permitted my case to go to the jury, there isn't the slightest doubt in my mind that I would have won their verdict.

The judge dismissed the twelve men and women with instructions that they not talk about the case. They filed past me, some with tears in their eyes, signaling their sympathy by their expressions or with a simple shake of the head.

But more specific evidence of how I would have fared had the jury been allowed to decide came to my attention several months later. An actor friend was in Macy's at Christmas time, watching a man demonstrate a new toy. They got into a conversation and my friend mentioned he was in the theater. The demonstrator asked if he happened to know an actor named Joe Julian. When told he did, the man confided that he was one of the jurors on my case. "Julian sure got a raw deal," he said. "Everyone on the jury was for him."

After the trial, Hays invited my wife and me to his magnificent Sands Point estate for a weekend of rest, swimming, and games of chess far into the night. It seemed to refresh him, and dilute the despair I brought with me from the courtroom. A prime slice of nature can go a long way toward putting problems into proper perspective. I wondered if his invitation was a consolation prize awarded all his clients who lost in court.

Yet in a very practical sense I didn't lose by my legal action. It actually cleared me for work in many areas where I had been blacklisted, because not only did the defendants make no real effort to further smear my name, but their main defense had been that I was one of those referred to in the small-print disclaimer in *Red Channels'* foreword, which stated that there might also be some "innocents" listed.

The ad agencies that began to call me again seemed glad to have even this negative sanction of my employability. With so many skilled radio actors on blacklists, it had become difficult to cast shows.

On the whole, I believe the broadcasting industry had wanted me to win my case. The agencies were opposed to blacklisting, although they rigidly practiced it. It was simple economics: they preferred losing good actors to good accounts. It was a rare sponsor that didn't succumb to the threat of boycott by the pressure groups. The agencies were caught in the middle. But if the networks had shown some backbone, blacklisting would not have succeeded as it did.

Blacklisting also became a profession—a money-making proposition. The publishers of *Red Channels* worked both sides of the street. They urged the firing of actors in the book, and at the same time offered "investigative services." For a fee, they reported to employers on the background of present or prospective employees. Five dollars was their minimum for a single, positive report. If it were negative, and the individual had a long history of associations with various organizations, the charge could be as high as a thousand dollars. The CBS network commissioned one study of program talent. Other clients were

General Motors, Du Pont, F. W. Woolworth, Metropolitan Life Insurance, R. J. Reynolds Tobacco, and Bendix Aviation.

Vincent Hartnett, who compiled and wrote the introduction to *Red Channels*, opened a commercial shop of his own. He acknowledged having received three hundred dollars for a report on playwright Arthur Miller, and two hundred dollars each in eight other instances. In 1955, just one client, Borden, the dairy-products company, is reported to have paid him ten thousand dollars.

Hartnett attended every day of my court proceedings as a spectator. Whenever I glanced at him he was busy scribbling notes. As soon as Saypol dismissed the jury, he came over and handed me his card, saying, "Joe, I want you to know you're all right with me. If you want to be helped, give me a call."

My thoughts were murderous.

He said he was getting out another book, an enlarged book, and that my name was also in that—but for other things.

It took a great effort to keep from punching him in the face. "What other things?" I seethed.

"Marching in the May Day Parade," he said.

That was all I needed. At a moment like that, with Saypol's judgment still ringing in my ears. I made a clenched fist. "I've never been in a May Day Parade in my life!" I shouted.

He patted his briefcase. "I have proof," he said. "In here."

He backed away as reporters crowded around. "I'll show Joe," he said. "Not you fellows."

I followed him to a side room, where he opened his case

and dumped a large pile of assorted snapshots on a conference table.

He sorted through them, then plucked out a small one showing a section of a parade. He tapped his finger triumphantly on a marching man in the middle of a crowd, a man about my size, about my weight, holding high a placard. You couldn't tell if his face resembled mine. The placard hid it. That should tell you something about Vincent Hartnett.

His apartment was said to be filled from top to bottom with cross-indexed files on actors, and huge piles of back-issue magazines and newspapers of all political colors, from which he industriously culled items that connected actors, in even the remotest way, to any organization with the slightest liberal tinge. In effect, this burrowing little fanatic, and a few others like him, decided which performers America could hear on their radio sets and which it couldn't. They were the powers to whom agencies would submit cast lists for a check on their political cleanliness. Apparently this was more discreet and convenient than to develop their own research apparatus, and worth the fees paid.

Has a note of bitterness crept into the account of my blacklisted years and the trial? After twenty years I should have been able to submerge it, and sift from the experience one of my golden philosophical nuggets, such as, "The innocent also get clobbered in this life." But philosophy isn't always adequate. And so to a generation that has not experienced the nightmare of that "blacklisting" period, when fear and hysteria enveloped the country, I simply want to say: Beware; it could happen again.

The biggest impetus for my "clearance" came from William Fitelson, a theatrical lawyer and executive producer of the *Theater Guild—U.S. Steel Hour* television series.

For a couple of years Fitelson had been intrigued with my play about the gift of the Japanese girl, and had tried to persuade U.S. Steel and its advertising agency, Batten, Barton, Durstine and Osborn, to produce it. But Steel would have none of anyone in *Red Channels*. After the trial, Fitelson tried again. This time I was invited to lunch at the Yale Club and grilled (no pun intended) by some agency officials, including their chief security officer, Jack Wren, a mysterious figure who seemed to be involved in many clearance situations.

They questioned me closely about my political thinking. Would I ransack my memory for any early activities or associations that might embarrass them if they put my play on the air? They had to be triply sure it would in no way contribute to the violent overthrow of our government. A few days later I was notified that Clifford F. Hood, the president of the United States Steel Corporation, had personally decided that the company would gamble on me.

Presento went on the air on December 16, 1954. There was no fallout. It was a critical and popular success. And the government was still intact.

That show broke the ice for me. Even though I didn't appear in it, the large credit as author that flashed on the screen gave notice to the industry. It said, in effect, that if I were safe enough to work for U.S. Steel, I should be safe enough for anyone.

The very next day I began getting calls for radio acting jobs.

13. Easy Money

But I had a lot of catching up to do. The jobs didn't come as thick and fast as before the "eclipse." Also, by the early fifties, television had finally come of age and was giving network radio a real run for the sponsors' money. Nonetheless, radio continued to command the lion's share of audiences. In 1954, 53,000,000 American homes had radios—and most had two or three; more than 130,000,000 sets were in use in the mid-fifties. And in spite of television's rapid growth, NBC launched a lavish ninety-minute weekly variety radio program. It was built around Tallulah Bankhead as hostess and Meredith Wilson as musical director. Each week it featured the biggest stars in show business.

Many movie stars were picking up quick, easy money guest starring on radio programs. It took little of their time; there was no costume or makeup problem; and it kept their names alive between films. On the whole, they weren't good—especially those who were stars more through personality and topography than talent. They knew nothing of microphone technique and did little more than read the words, with varying degrees of intelligence. The supporting casts of radio actors acted rings around them.

I once played opposite Veronica Lake in a Broadway theater that had been converted to radio use. As legitimate theater declined, a number of these houses were taken over, and radio shows were put on before live audiences. *The Theater Guild on the Air* was one. These productions generated extra excitement for the actors. They gave us a feeling of being back in the theater. We usually dressed— tux and evening gowns—and the live audience reaction gave listeners at home a sense of participating in an important theatrical event.

On this show with Miss Lake the engineer had a problem. Hers was such a weak, wispy voice that he couldn't get us in proper balance. So he gave her a separate microphone across the stage from me, where he could mechanically raise her voice level to mine. Which was fine for the listeners at home. In the studio, her voice was still small, and now so far from me I had to strain to hear my cues. Especially since they had her facing front so the audience could see her famous peek-a-boo hairdo. Hardly the way to play an intimate love scene with a lady!

And there was Myrna Loy. An actress of great dignity and charm, who had won a special place in the Hollywood firmament and in my young, tender, movie-going heart. For years I had been intrigued by the mysterious emanations of this lovely lady—always with that slight enigmatic smile that suggested she knew more than she was telling. She was so thin, though. I really used to worry about her health.

And then one day, there she was, in studio 3G at NBC, life-size, and playing a scene with *me!* It was a deep, corny thrill.

But if she had had to win that role in a competitive audition with radio actresses, she wouldn't have been there. Her voice, isolated from her other attributes, was dull and flat. She was selling her name, not her art. Still, big film names did attract listeners no matter how they sounded. When shows were live, it was a little like their making a personal appearance—except you were only hearing them. And you drew on your memory of how they looked.

Marlene Dietrich, on the other hand, had something more to sell than her name. She had a famous, throaty, sexy voice, and was a true professional in whatever medium she sold her commodities.

Her career included several radio series. One was an *Advice to the Lovelorn* program, where she personally wrote the answers to letters she read on the air. Another was a series of romantic dramas called *Time for Love.* And there was *Café Istanbul*—a weekly spy format that took audiences into the casbah and other mysterious places. It was a program well calculated to exploit her exotic accent and strong voice-presence.

Working with her occasionally on *Café Istanbul*, I got a glimpse behind the public image of Marlene Dietrich—a woman of strength, warmth, and intelligence, yet so spontaneous that when, during a rehearsal, she overheard one of the actors express doubt that the rest of her body was as youthful as her famous legs, she ripped open her blouse to prove him wrong.

She concerned herself with every aspect of a production. Especially casting. After the show had been on the air a while and she became familiar with the pool of available radio actors, she had definite ideas about who should be cast in which part.

One week she told Murray Burnett, the writer-director, that she wanted a certain actor for the male lead. When told he was out of town, she insisted he be tracked down. When informed he had had a nervous breakdown and was in an institution upstate, she insisted he be gotten out. Burnett phoned the authorities and urged them to release him for the one day. He argued that it would be therapeutic for the actor to know he was still wanted professionally. It was a convincing argument and they agreed. Burnett drove up in his car, picked him up, and took full responsibility for returning him the next day.

There was a slight problem—solved by the miracle of newly-developed magnetic tape. The actor was one of radio's best, but he was under such heavy sedation that his reflexes were slowed and it seemed forever before he picked up his cues. But since this show was taped it was possible, with a little sensitive surgery, to snip out the long pauses and restore the pace of a good performance.

Most of the high-powered Hollywood stars of the period acted in radio, and at one time or another, I worked with James Stewart, Henry Fonda, Edward G. Robinson, Claude Raines, Rudy Vallee, Barbara Stanwyck, Walter Huston, Tyrone Power, Boris Karloff, Tallulah Bankhead, and Frank Sinatra.

From October 6, 1953, to March 30, 1954, Sinatra did a weekly half-hour private-eye show on NBC called *Rocky Fortune*.

From time to time I had been told that, from a certain angle, I resembled Sinatra. I told him that once. I said,

"Frank, a lot of people tell me I look like you. Do a lot of people tell you you look like me?" He said no.

We rehearsed one morning, then broke for lunch, to report back in an hour for further rehearsal and recording. Sinatra didn't return; even his manager was baffled. We waited several hours. Finally he phoned—wouldn't say from where—and told his manager to pay the actors and let them go. This was during a period he seemed to be having problems with himself.

14. Foot-in-Mouth Disease

As technologies developed, many radio shows were recorded for later broadcast—first on wax, then on glass disks, then on acetate, then on wire, and then tape. But radio was at its best "live." The "aliveness"—the knowledge that something could always go wrong—greatly heightened the appeal. Awareness that "this is it"— millions listening, no retakes, no redress of error, no second chance—created a tension, an extra edge of excitement in performers that communicated to listeners.

It also gave some performers and announcers such a bad case of nerves that they lost control of their speech. The often hilarious consequences were known as bloopers. Blooper collections from both radio and TV are gathered as assiduously today as vases from the Ming Dynasty, and are traded between collectors throughout the country.

Of course, they are much funnier to hear than read, but here are a few that I've collected through the years. Probably the most famous was the time radio announcer Harry Von Zell, covering the inauguration of President Herbert Hoover over a nationwide network, announced:

208

Ladies and gentlemen, I now give you the President of the United States, Hoobert Heever. Er . . . Heevert Hoober—I mean Hovert Haber!

Since then, all announcers who introduce the Chief Executive are required to merely announce: "Ladies and gentlemen, the President of the United States."

Then there was the sportscaster who said:

"Sports fans! Stay stewed for the Stupor Bowl."

And the announcer who introduced Bennet Cerf as "a well-known author and lecherer."

And the actor playing a doctor, who said in a low, tense voice:

"Nurse, a hypodeemic nurdle, please."

And the nervous juvenile who, when his girl friend's mother answered the doorbell, blurted out:

"I've c-called to come on your daughter."

And announcers who said:

Girls, when you have to get up early to prepare his breakfast, do you wake up feeling lustless—I mean, listless?

This portion of the *Name of the Gum* starring Robert Stick—er Stack—is brought to you by Wrigley's Chewing Game.

Marshall Dillon preserves law and odor tonight on *Gunsmoke.*

This portion of *I Dream of Jeannie* is brought to you by Vick's Navel Spray.

We now switch you to the sixteenth tee, where we show you in slow motion Arnold Palmer, U.S. Opium Champion.

And the forecast for tomorrow is mostly Sunday.

Don't be a litterbird. Join Ladybug Johnson and help clean up America.

Jackie Kennedy returned today from her African visit bringing with her a whale's tool * for a souvenir.

Copywriters make their own bloopers, without the excuse of "microphone nerves." But they must have had alibis for writing copy like:

And so ends another garden tip program. Tune in next week, when Mrs. Van Buren's topic will be "My Potted Friends."

Try this remarkably effective cough syrup. We guarantee you'll never get any better.

At Johnson's Laundry, we don't tear your clothes by machine, we do it carefully by hand.

See Lassie in three parts after this message from the Anti-Vivisection League.

And some that looked all right on the page, but conveyed a different thought when spoken fluently by the announcer. A classic example of this genre:

Why not give your wife a gorgeous Gruen for Christmas?

The remarkable thing about written bloopers is that they got by so many people. Every syllable of commercial copy had to be approved by the sponsor, the legal department of the radio station, the advertising agency, the production department, the artistic department, etc. By the time it reached the studio, it was too sacrosanct to tamper with, and the announcer had to read it with a straight face. Very often he couldn't and "broke up." Audiences, too, get a kick out of hearing an announcer giggle his way through a

---

* Presumably, the announcer meant "tooth."

commercial, even though they don't always understand the reason for it. They know something is wrong behind the scenes and enjoy being even partly privy to it.

Many excellent performers, completely at ease on a stage, were terrified of a microphone. Luther Adler, one of the theater's finest, shook so badly on his first radio assignment that he read aloud from his script the words: "Low— nervous—" the directions preceding his dialogue.

Frequently an actor's trembling hand rattled the pages so close to the microphone that it came over sounding like a hurricane or a building collapsing, to the detriment of the scene and the chagrin of the control room engineer. (Another *bête noir* of the engineer was the belly growl—a sure laugh, especially if it happened on the air during a pause.)

Occasionally a hand was unsteady for a different reason. Although most announcers tried their best to sound inhuman (sonorous unction and flawless diction were the criteria), if you stuck them they bled and if they drank too much they got smashed, even as you and I—even a famous announcer whom I shall not identify, because why should I slur the good man's name? Anyway, he arrived in the studio so drunk his knees gave way as he began to introduce a program on the air and he collapsed to the floor. The cast rushed to lift him, but his two hundred pounds were too much. The situation was saved by an actor who had the presence of mind to grab the standing microphone and bring it down to the famous announcer, who bestirred himself from his prone position to lean on an elbow, and, squinting closely at his script, managed at least to finish the introduction—if not with perfect diction, at least fluff-lessly.

At the opposite end of the jitters spectrum was the most unflappable performer I have ever known: Jean Paul King, one of radio's top announcers in the late thirties and early forties. (I sometimes equate announcers with performers because they were often more than abstract voices that read the commercials and introduced and signed off the show. As regular guests in listeners' homes, they became familiar personalities. On many comedy shows they played foil for the star, and a number of them went on to become celebrities in their own right, such as Milton Cross, Durward Kirby, Jimmy Wallington, Ben Grauer, Bert Parks, etc.—each with his own distinctive trade mark of speech and personality.)

If one word were to describe Jean Paul King, it would be "smooth." Everything about him—his skin, his face, his hair, his speech, his manner—was smooth. Nothing fazed him while he was working. He was a marvelously efficient, nerveless announcing machine. With little or no study, he could pick up his script and read off a long commercial, written in impossibly stilted language and full of references to tongue-twisting, newly discovered "secret ingredients," wave hello to a friend who had just entered the studio, and finish without missing a beat.

Although awed by such perfect coordination of mind, body, and commercial, I used to find myself wishing he would make a mistake. Fluff, slur a word, or drop his pages. I like my heroes flawed. I felt a little like Toscanini the time he went to Jascha Heifetz's dressing room after a concert and begged him to play for him just one false note before he died.

One evening, during the famous reporter Floyd Gibbons' show *Headline Hunters* on NBC, something evil made me saunter up to the mike where King had just begun a long commercial about how a certain shampoo kills "Pitarosporimovali," a bacteria that causes a form of dandruff. I took a half dollar from my pocket and flipped it in front of his face. He glanced up, reached in his own pocket, pulled out another half dollar, pointed to himself then to me (signaling "I'll match you"), flipped the coin, caught it, slapped it on his forearm as I did with mine, won my half dollar, reached across the mike to collect, and finished the commercial without once violating the script, his style, rhythm, or aplomb. As I said—smooth.

Another example of professional *savoir-faire* was when the well-known announcer Norman Brokenshire was doing a show that, due to a timing error, finished five minutes too soon. Dead air being the cardinal sin of radio, Brokenshire saved the situation by announcing, "Ladies and gentlemen, we bring you the sounds of New York City!" He pulled open the studio window, thrust out the microphone, and held it there for the full five minutes.

Which reminds me of another lovely example of resourcefulness—this time an author's. For a time, the daily serial *The Road of Life* was heard over two major networks until the sponsor decided to eliminate NBC and play it only on CBS. The final day on both, the announcer's tag line read: Starting tomorrow, *The Road of Life* will be heard only over CBS.

This didn't sit well with NBC. It was bad enough losing the show, but a free plug for the rival network was rubbing it in. So they ordered it eliminated.

But the writer, Charles Gussman, a shrewd and determined fellow, rewrote the last scene as a phone conversation between Dr. Brent, the leading character, and a patient who was asking for an appointment. Brent responded by saying that he was moving the next day and could be reached only in care of Doctor C. B. Hess. On paper this was nothing NBC could object to. But spoken by actor Don MacLaughlin, who de-emphasized the word "doctor" and stressed the rest, it was exactly what Gussman wanted it to say. Sneaky, sneaky.

In the same department is the one about W. C. Fields, who, on a prime-time evening show, vexed his sponsor by continually adlibbing a reference to his nephew, Chester (Fields). The sponsor was a rival cigarette company.

Things often went wrong in radio. Remember lovable old Uncle Don, host of a children's show? He is alleged to have concluded a broadcast and sighed, "Well, that'll hold the little bastards," unaware that the engineer was a moment late in flicking a switch, thus permitting those immortal words to be heard from sea to shining sea.

There are those who deny this actually happened, and those who swear they heard it. But true or not, it could have happened. Goofs were to be expected in a medium that poured out shows in such abundance. They could be anything from suddenly discovering your pages were mixed up, having to run quickly to the other side of the mike, and read over another actor's shoulder, to what happened to a director named Jim Jewell, putting on an episode of *Jack Armstrong, the All American Boy*. He threw a cue so hard he smashed his fist through the glass panel separating him from the actors.

Or, in a scene where you're supposed to pull a gun and say, "I'm going to put a bullet through your heart," and the sound-effects man's gun jams, and he keeps trying and clicks and clicks it until you brilliantly adlib, "No! On second thought it will give me greater pleasure to choke you with my bare hands!"—and *then* the gun goes off.

The revolver jammed once during a performance of *The Shadow*. The director, Chick Vincent, was so upset he ran from the control room and shouted into the mike, "Bang! Bang!" It just seemed the right thing to do. The show fell apart as the cast dissolved in laughter.

Once during a broadcast before an audience from the New Amsterdam Roof (a converted Broadway theater) an actor with failing eyesight, in order not to lose his place, marked his script with colored pencils—one color for his dialogue, another for his cues. As the show went on the air, the amber stage lights were turned on the performers, washing out all the colored markings. The poor actor fluffed and panicked, and the scene went out the window.

Then there was the time when Broadway star Helen Menken, who was used to freedom of movement on the stage, flung her arm out in such an emphatic gesture that the back of her hand caught the actress next to her full in the face, causing her to yelp with pain and drop her pages.

Apropos adlibbing, Norman Rose, an actor-narrator noted for the deep, cello-toned resonance of his voice, once played Joseph in a dramatization of the biblical story of Joseph and his brothers. It was on a program called *The Eternal Light* (still on the air over NBC). Joseph was thrown into a deep pit by his brothers. The director instructed Norman to adlib for them to take him out. On the air, when the cue came, he spontaneously yelled, "Jesus Christ, get me out of here!" The story took place, of course, several centuries before Christ's birth and, to make matters worse, the show was sponsored by the Jewish Theological Seminary.

Constantly expecting the unexpected created tensions that often found release in horseplay and practical jokes. Engineers were frequently given a hard time by a performer who looked up at the glass-enclosed control room and silently mouthed words as though he were talking to him. The puzzled engineer, not hearing any sound, checked all his wires, plugs, and controls, thinking something was wrong with his equipment. If such tomfoolery occurred just before going on the air, he would be really frantic. That was mean.

Another mean one (confined usually to rehearsals) was to saunter up to the mike with a cigarette lighter and casually set a top corner of an announcer's page on fire. This had the effect of speeding his tempo.

One morning I was doing a recording of *Boston Blackie* ("Enemy to those who make him an enemy; friend to those who have no friends!"). The title role was played by Richard Kollmar, who, with his wife, Dorothy Kilgallen, were the Dorothy and Dick of WOR's early morning "breakfast" talk show of the same name.

Halfway through the first reading, I found my dialogue difficult to understand. I asked the director, Jeanne Harrison, who was in the control room, if she could clarify it for me. She brusquely told me to go on with the reading. I tried, but it was impossible. I'd acted in some awful scripts in my time, but this was absolute nonsense. The words bogged down in hopeless *non sequiturs*. I began to laugh. Larry Haines, the actor playing the scene with me, tried hard to suppress his titters. Miss Harrison turned nasty. I had never seen her that way before.

"You're not here to criticize the script!" she snapped. "You're here to play it!"

I tried again, but there was just no way of phrasing those words. She kept at me. I felt a rage rising.

"You're supposed to be an actor, aren't you? Well, then act!" she blustered, her voice coming over the talkback, blaring and raucous.

"This stuff is unplayable!" I exploded.

"Do as you're told!" she shouted.

"Nobody can play this crap!" I yelled.

"That's what you're being paid for!" she screamed. "If you can't do it, I'll get someone who can!"

"Go ahead, goddammit!" I said, in full fury. "I don't have to take this kind of abuse from you!" I slammed my script down on the floor, grabbed my hat and coat, and started out.

At this point the entire cast burst out laughing. Jeanne came out of the control room, embraced me and confessed it was all a setup. Those "impossible" pages of the script had been deliberately inserted to provoke my reaction. They had recorded my frustration and the entire explosive scene between us—to play next morning on *Dorothy and Dick*.

My frayed feelings were calmed by an extra fee.

Probably the best-known practical joke was the one Orson Welles pulled on Charles Martin—the same Charles Martin who testified at my trial. Martin directed an episode of the *Philip Morris Playhouse;* Welles narrated.

Tensely waiting for Martin's cue to speak, as the hand of the studio clock approached air time, Welles suddenly dropped his script and the pages scattered over the floor. None of the other actors moved to help him recover them.

Martin himself frantically ran from the control room, got down on his hands and knees, desperately scooped up all the pages, hurriedly collated and thrust them up to Welles, just as the red ON THE AIR sign flashed. Welles calmly shoved them aside, pulled the real script from his pocket, and began his narration on time.

Incidentally, if an actor on the *Philip Morris Playhouse* was seen smoking a rival brand of cigarette, it could cost him his job. The same on other shows sponsored by tobacco companies, such as *The Camel Caravan, The Old Gold Show,* and *The Lucky Strike Hit Parade.* In the studio, you dared flash only a pack of the sponsor's cigarettes. This situation was frequently met by throwing away the original contents and refilling the pack with your own favorite brand.

A similar prank was pulled on orchestra leader Richard Himber by his musicians and production staff, who conspired to set the studio clock five minutes ahead. When ON THE AIR flashed and the director gave the cue to bring in the music, Himber was the only one who didn't know they weren't really on the air. When his musicians deliberately played sour notes, he writhed in agony. He glared and grimaced and made threatening gestures with his baton, but the musicians kept missing cues and making musical clinkers until Himber's torture became unbearable. Then they all stopped playing and laughed.

There was a lot of fun and lighthearted camaraderie among the "in" radio people of those days—much of it, I believe, because most busy actors didn't take themselves too seriously. Once they developed a technique they could rely on, they often felt free during a performance to read a book, or newspaper, or play gin rummy until their cue came up.

And certain programs were fun to do. Like a Corwin show, or *The Goldbergs*. Gertrude Berg liked to set up a little *mise en scène*, and have her actors work their own sound effects, whenever possible, such as knocking on and opening and closing doors. If it were a dinner scene, she'd have us sitting around a table, rattling our own cups and saucers. It improved our timing and gave us a feeling of full-dimensional acting.

I also enjoyed working the big nighttime variety shows with the famous comedians: Fred Allen, Milton Berle, Ed Gardner of *Duffy's Tavern*, Robert Q. Lewis, etc. They usually did sketches manufactured each week by a stable of high-powered (and high-priced) writers, whose talent was measured mostly by the size of their cross-indexed files. Their brains were full of jokes. Mention any subject and they'd instantly produce a stream of relevant gags. They were masters of the old switcheroo; take an old one and give it a new twist. Craftsmen of the topper and the topper of the topper. Many have gone on to glory elsewhere—Neil Simon, Abe Burrows, and yes, Herman Wouk. These shows were nearly always done before large studio audiences, whose laughter improved the actors and made the job fun, and you even got paid for it.

Funniest fun for me was *The Fred Allen Show*. Allen was more than a comedian, he was a rare wit, and wrote much of his material himself. He had a variety of guests, but the most famous feature of his show was *Allen's Alley*—sketches performed by a little stock company of characters with wonderful names like "Senator Claghorn," "Pansy Nussbaum," "Titus Moody," "Socrates Mulligan," "Falstaff Openshaw," and a Chinese detective, "One Long Pan."

One of the favorite targets of Allen's sharp satire was the network officials themselves, with whom he was constantly at war over their efforts to tone down his material. They couldn't bleep out what they didn't like because shows were live in those days. Their only recourse was to cut him off the air at the first hint of objectionable material—which they did a number of times.

Another network practice that infuriated Allen was cutting the show off the air at precisely the last second of allotted time. Comedy shows were hard to time accurately because of the unpredictability of the studio audience's laughter and would occasionally run over a number of seconds. Finally, on one show Allen channeled his anger into the following dialogue between himself and his wife, Portland, who was a regular on the program:

PORTLAND: Why were you cut off last Sunday?
ALLEN: Who knows? The main thing in radio is to come out on time. If people laugh, the program is longer. The thing to do is to get a nice dull half hour. Nobody will laugh or applaud. Then you'll always be right on time, and all of the little emaciated radio executives can dance around their desks in interoffice abandon.
PORTLAND: Radio sure is funny.
ALLEN: All except the comedy programs. Our program has been cut off so many times the last page of the script is a Band-Aid.
PORTLAND: What does the network do with all the time it saves cutting off the ends of programs?

ALLEN: Well, there is a big executive here at the network. He is the vice-president in charge of "Ah! Ah! You're running too long!" He sits in a little glass closet with his mother-of-pearl gong. When your program runs overtime he thumps his gong with a marshmallow he has tied to the end of a xylophone stick. Bong! You're off the air. Then he marks down how much time he's saved.

PORTLAND: What does he do with all this time?

ALLEN: He adds it all up—ten seconds here, twenty seconds there—and when he has saved up enough seconds, minutes, and hours to make two weeks, the network lets the vice-president use the two weeks of your time for his vacation.

Halfway through this sketch was cut off the air.

I was on Allen's show once as a guest star. You see, I have an odd little talent that intrigues people (not all), and every once in a while I was invited to demonstrate it on a show. Actually, it is quite an accomplishment. Unbelievable. Absolutely incredible. Fabulous. I am able to produce a musical tone by clasping my two palms together and slowly pulling them apart. By controlling the sound with other hand muscles, I can squeeze out musical compositions. Many find this hilarious, others revolting. True, I have never quite been able to refine it to the point of touching people aesthetically, but the tunes are recognizable—even some classical pieces—and the effect quite startling. You really have to hear it to know what I'm talking about.

Anyhow, I was invited to "play my hands" on Fred Allen's program. That evening was one of my fondest radio memories. I thought I had heard every possible joke about my hands, but Allen sprang a few new ones. "What kind of music are you going to palm off on us tonight?" he asked. "Handel?" and after I played "Swanee River": "If you put mittens on, would that be like muting a trombone?"

Although the sound itself was just this side of vulgar, amplification and (blush) artistry made it funny. The studio audience howled.

However, like every great artist, I wasn't completely satisfied with my work. I felt I could have squeezed out a purer tone if my hands hadn't perspired. Now, in those days, because of the time difference, we had to come back at midnight to do a repeat show for the West Coast. During the interval I went out and bought myself some talcum powder in order to keep my "instrument" dry. As I was being introduced on the air, I took the can from my pocket and dusted my hands. Allen, right across the mike from me, hadn't seen this on the first show, and I had neglected to warn him. He broke up. He guffawed so loudly into the mike—which was wide open for my tiny little squeak—that he knocked us off the air. I can't explain that technically, but I swear it happened.

After my guest appearance, I received an interesting fan letter:

> 10 Mountnoel Ave.,
> Toronto, Ont.
> Canada.

Mr. Hand Musicmaker
Dear Sir,

I heard you on Fred Allen's show tonight and thought I would like to tell you that I have a habit of doing the same thing for which you were on Fred's program for.

I acquired it as a nervous habit also and up to this time it has been looked upon with disapproving eyes by my parents. At the time of your act though a change has come into their stare and it is now of a sort of reverence.

It struck me so funny that I couldn't help writing you this note.

Hoping that I can make music like you I will close.

Yours respectfully,
D.E.

It pleased me to have contributed to the serenity of his home life, but it was saddening to learn I was no longer unique.

Leonard Lyons, the syndicated columnist for the *New York Post,* once had me demonstrate my extraordinary talent for the famous impresario, Sol Hurok. Hurok was greatly amused, but for some reason never asked how to get in touch with me.

Another time Lyons introduced me to the great pianist Artur Rubinstein and told him of my musical gift. Rubinstein asked me to play something for him. I squeaked out a bit of "The Hall of the Mountain King" from Grieg's *Peer Gynt*. He was delighted. "Ach," he said, with elaborate gestures, "that is wonderful! You are so full of music it comes out your fingers!" and then added, "I still need a piano."

My thirty years of radio activity pretty well spanned the spectrum—from the foolishness with my hands to playing Hamlet. Somewhere along the line, I touched nearly all bases—including sound-effects man, announcer, newscaster, disk jockey, writer, and foreign correspondent.

Throughout it all, I stubbornly clung to the notion that

this was not really my career, only a temporary way of making a living until I connected with the right role and made it big in the theater, or Hollywood.

How long is temporary? Lord, how fooled we mortals be. I don't know at what point I stopped thinking of radio as marking time; perhaps I never did—even after 20,000 broadcasts. But the fact is that during those thirty years a full-fledged career budded and blossomed, for which I'm enormously grateful. It was a privilege to have been there during the salad days of radio—to have participated in the dynamic growth of this potent medium and art form that rewarded me with adventures, that deepened and enriched my life.

Would the theater have sent me to opposite ends of the earth to report the condition of man under the ultimate stress of war? Hardly.

Would the theater have allowed me to play Hamlet? Methinks nay.

Or leading man to such glamorous stars of my childhood as Marlene Dietrich, Fay Wray, Myrna Loy, Joan Crawford, Nancy Carrol, Veronica Lake, Helen Hayes—to name-drop only a little? Unlikely. Although not strictly a character type I'm just off center enough not to be thought of as a romantic lead. But in radio I was assigned them constantly.

In this regard, radio was a boon to many frustrated actors whose physical qualities didn't quite match their leading-man souls. Six foot tall and symmetrical didn't matter. Of course, they couldn't be too misshapen, either, because then it had to do with the actor's image of himself. If he couldn't believe, the audience wouldn't. And so, actually, most of radio's leading men and women looked the part.

Although in many cases the audience imagined them more handsome than they were.

What a wondrous thing was that imagination. How real it made a radio drama—especially a soap opera, where five days a week, year in and year out, millions of women listened as they did their housework, deeply identifying with the characters in all their joys and suffering—mostly suffering.

In the theater, or at the movies, or when we read a novel, we know it's not real, but we suspend our disbelief. In radio it was astonishing how many listeners had no disbelief to suspend.

Once, on *The Life of Mary Sothern*, the character I was playing got married. I received numerous wedding presents in the mail, including baby clothes and a bassinet.

When on *The O'Neills* I played the role of a man being tried for a murder he did not commit, and it was very sad because he had no money to hire a good lawyer, several listeners were so moved that they mailed in money to start a defense fund.

I've often wondered if people had to be a little cracked to believe so profoundly in the reality of those soap operas. I'm still not sure of the answer.

We all have an innate will to believe. Our capacity to do so has been eroded by the exploiters of our innocence, but I suspect there are those who have hung on to the purity of their naïveté and believe everything they see, read, or hear. Orson Welles' famous *War of the Worlds* broadcast is a good example of the credulity out there in radio land, not only because the nation panicked when told the Martians had invaded. In this age of enlightened science, the most sophisticated can keep a corner of his mind open to that possibility. What interested me was that even after the country was told that it was only a radio show, for weeks people drove by to get a tourist's thrill out of staring at the spot in New Jersey where the Martians were supposed to have landed.

Cracked? I prefer to think of them as pure in heart.

15. Fan Mail

Fan mail played a large part in the lives of radio performers.

Most fan mail was received by those who played running parts. We didn't hear our applause, but we read it. And it strengthened us. Often radio actors had the funny feeling they were just sending words out into a cosmic vacuum. Letters received from "out there" confirmed our function.

Fan letters to radio stars differed from most movie fan mail. The intimacy of the medium seemed to invite more intimate letters. And though most were complimentary, there was no typical fan. They came in all fabrics. Some were flirtatious:

> . . . I have an idea you are about twenty-two, someone who likes tweeds and smokes a pipe. Maybe you have blond, wavy hair with blue eyes or maybe you don't but that's what I want to find out. Would you *please* send me a picture?
>
> Your's truly till next Monday at 8:30.

. . . I listen to *Big Sister* religiously. However, I don't know whether I have a crush on "Ken Morgan" or Joe Julian—or both. Probably it is the composite man, at that. I'm sure it was your voice I heard on one of *Aunt Jenny's Real Life Stories*, in which you played the husband, "John," and I was taken with you then, too, so maybe it is Joe Julian after all. A photograph will soon set me straight, because if it doesn't compare favorably with the picture I have in my mind of "Ken Morgan," I shall go back to being faithful to the latter, and no more questions asked about the real man—he can go hang.

Some needed to tell their problems:

I first became interested in these daytime serials some months ago when I found myself living alone with my baby, and practically housebound taking care of him. He is now ten months old and naturally I am still more or less confined to my home looking after him so that dialing in the daytime shows has become at least a habit, if not actually part of my existence . . .

They were all ages:

. . . I am listening to you now and drawing all over the paper at the same time. You were wonderful on the *Inner Sanctum*, but why do you have to be a murderer?

. . . My girlfriend Margaret Smith and me have listened to you on *Nero Wolfe* and we want your photograph. I hope the program will still be on when we go back to school and that mother will let me stay up to hear it.

Anyway here is five cents for the picture. We are buying defense stamps but will send more if you want it.

Some were critical:

Dear Archie:

This letter is an appeal to you to save my respect for Nero Wolfe. Have you ever heard him express pleasure in any way except by a heavy throated laugh? He's so nonchalant in working with his orchids and discussing good food and solving all those mysteries that I cannot imagine him spending so much energy in bringing forth that awful laugh. As his assistant, can't you *do* something about it? Best wishes for success in this matter.

Some were angry:

. . . We Catholics of Salt Lake City take strong exception to the remarks of Joseph Julian in *An American Back Home* over KSL, in which he says the Nazi cause won out in the revolt of the religious people of Spain against the liberal government which was repudiated by the people. The people are happy now they have a liberal dictatorship. Everybody in Spain knows what started the revolt—the murder of 17,000 priests, the burning of 16,000 churches, hundreds of convents destroyed and nuns raped and holy men killed who had never done anybody any wrong and who had never turned a hungry person from their gates. I defy smart aleck correspondents like Joseph Julian who know nothing about God and who largely get their information sitting around hotel lobbies to disprove these figures! . . .

Some were consoling:

. . . Am I correct in recognizing in the *David Harum* story, the creator of the original Michael West?

We were disappointed when someone else took your place, because we felt that no one else would ever be quite suitable in a role that you had created and incidentally, we no longer listen to this story . . .

And some were deeply grateful:

. . . I listened to your delightful *American in England* program every week. They are so very human and lifelike. You see, I am an Englishwoman, born, raised, and married in England. I came to this country as a bride in 1918. My good husband is an American and he was a soldier in the last World War.

Now my fine and dear son is somewhere in this war. He is a lieutenant and twenty-three and a law graduate of the University of Minnesota. We haven't heard from him in over two months, so we are sad and longing to hear that he is safe and still well. . . .

My family back home lost all by bombs, but they did not kick any. They showed such a fine spirit.

Please carry on with your programs.

Many of us answered our own fan mail, which often led to long-term pen relationships, usually with shut-ins, for whom these contacts were golden treasures.

16. Whither Withered Radio?

What was radio? It was, actually, a rather silly-looking spectacle: a group of unglamorous people sitting or strolling around a large room, holding sheets of paper in their hands, mumbling to themselves; going up to a microphone, delivering their lines, sitting down, lighting a cigarette. A grown man jumps up and down in a sandbox creating the sound of running footsteps, or slaps his chest for horses' hoofbeats, or slowly crushes the cellophane wrapper from a pack of cigarettes to indicate a forest fire, while behind a glass panel, a man with a worried look on his face and a stop watch in his hand makes "stretch" or "faster" signs for the performers, who then change pace according to the purchased piece of time rather than the dictates of artistic imperative.

But, miraculously, all this nonsense came out the other end fused in a concord of sounds that gripped, entertained, and enthralled millions of Americans every day. Radio drama was the tranquilizer, the emotional pain-killing drug of the time. The profound depths of its influence on the national psyche will never be known, but the ubiquitous murder mysteries, the simplistic action dramas, and the moist soap operas at least made life more bearable for the isolated, the lonely, and the frustrated, who, by identifying with the characters, daily achieved some degree of catharsis—which, I submit, is a proper function of art.

The audience experience was unique in another important way. Television and film audiences are essentially passive. They watch and wait for something to be "done" to them. Theater audiences, too, mainly relate passively to happenings on stage—in spite of the "liveness" and the three-cornered current that flows among ourselves, the actors, and other members of the audience. But radio is "Theater in the Mind," and the audience must earn its reward. It must always expend energy, reaching out to embellish, to supply what is not there. It is a private, personal medium, best listened to at home with no distractions to the exercise of imagination.

No other art form ever engaged the imagination more intensely. Even bad radio shows were better than their equivalent in other media, the listener's imagination providing more reality than could be shown on a screen or stage. This creative expenditure of energy made the listeners collaborators in the truest sense. They designed the costumes and created the scenery. They visualized nuances of locale and performance that the writer didn't write and the actor couldn't convey. This, I believe, accounts for the great nostalgia—for the glowing affection with which those of you who are old enough remember your favorite radio programs. Because they were, largely, your own creations.

So why did it die? If radio was so wonderful, why did it

dwindle down to music and news, disk jockies and phoned-in questions to experts who know everything about everything?

As television developed, the big advertising budgets were shifted into this new, exciting, visual medium, with its fantastic selling potential. You could make viewers drool for products by *showing* them! Radio became a stepchild. Especially radio drama.

But something funny happened on the way to the poorhouse. The radio networks, in changing their format, discovered they could make as much money without hiring actors, producers, writers, directors and musicians to put on dramas. The one-man shows saved them a bundle. And they sold even more commercials. The talk shows squeeze them in almost between syllables—which can't be done on a structured dramatic program.

And so, like it or not, for over a decade the public has been deprived of an art form that flourishes in every other major country in the world.

But hark! I hear a crackle of static! And isn't that Orson Welles' voice, laughing maniacally as The Shadow? And that burst of machine-gun fire and the screaming siren? Why that's the old *Gangbusters* signature! And there's the *Inner Sanctum* door squeaking open? And wasn't that Molly telling Fibber, "Tain't funny, McGee"?

Do I really hear this or am I hallucinating?

No, it's for real. The corpse is stirring. Someone bought up recordings of these oldies and gave them a ride over 500 FM stations around the country.

Discovery! Wow, this stuff's great! The kids love it! They've never known anything like it! And for the old folks—nostalgia! The whole country's on a nostalgia kick!

Well, that's only a fad, it will soon pass. Ah but no! Commercial nostrils are quivering. And here is Hi Brown with an idea whose time has come—again.

For years Brown had been working to bring back radio drama, pitching low-budget packages at the networks and getting regular turndowns. Now was the time, if ever. By finding more corners to cut, such as winning concessions from the actors' union, lining up writers for $300 a script with instructions to keep the casts small, he was able to offer the networks a low cost, modern version of *Inner Sanctum,* squeaking door and all, with E. G. Marshall as host.

CBS, sniffing out this wind from the past, decided to gamble. They made a deal for an hour network show every day for a year.

The response to this show—the *CBS Mystery Theatre*— was enormous. It gave major impetus to the upswing now in the making.* Love stories, soap operas, and westerns are being planned. Rod Serling began hosting the *Hollywood Radio Mystery Theater,* produced on the West Coast and syndicated across the country. The FM Stations (the Off-Broadway of radio) are already carrying a number of new programs such as the *National Lampoon Radio Hour,* with sketches more daringly satirical than anything in the past, and heard on over 100 stations. An all-black soap opera is in production.

How far this revival will go I don't know. Certainly our

---

* The first ratings showed that this program, in the New York area alone, is garnering the largest total audience—approximately a quarter million listeners per one quarter hour—virtually twice the audience of the second place station, and equal to the combined totals of its two closest competitors.

passion for radio will never again be such that movie houses interrupt their films, as they used to do, to bring their audiences the latest chapter of *Amos and Andy* over the public-address system. Radio will never regain its pre-television eminence. But to realize even its potential, it must go beyond the "oldies" and old concepts. It can't get stuck in nostalgia. It must deal with conflicts that reflect the life and problems of today.

But who will write the scripts? There are still a few radio writers around, but they're mostly too old and set in their thinking. Fresh young minds and talents are needed to speak for now. But where are they? With practically no radio drama around for more than a decade, where could they have developed a writing technique?

They must start from scratch. Trial and error. As in the beginning. And the industry must nurture them. Experimental programs are needed where they can get a start, and perhaps, incubate some quality shows above the "pulp" level. Minority tastes must also be catered to. If radio drama is to have a continuing place in broadcasting, the whole body must be revived. So let's also hear it for shows with some cultural protein. Let's hear it for the art houses of the "Theater in the Mind." Maybe there's another Norman Corwin out there somewhere. Let's shout him a word of encouragement. Or how about the original? Maybe, if we shout loud enough we can entice him back, convince the network moguls to commission him some new work—or ask them to revive some old Corwin.

What about the performing talent? Where are today's microphone-trained actors? We needn't worry. Supply will catch up with the demand. They'll come out of the woodwork if the need is there, including the specialists, the screamers, animal imitators, and baby criers. Those with the knack will just need a little time to develop.

If you're wondering what happened to that great pool of marvelously skilled performers of the past, some have died, some retired, some managed to cross the bridge to films, television and the stage, and the rest are out a'whorin' in commercials. Many became rich using their microphone training to do radio and voice-over (off-camera) commercials. And since their income now depends on how well they sell products, they rightfully take more pride in their accomplishments as salesmen than as actors. Well, there have always been periods in history when art put itself in the service of commerce. And if there are still any foolish idealists among us who feel that actors should nourish the human spirit more directly than by selling Mrs. Jones a product that waxes her floors better, or Mr. Jones a bottle of something that improves his breath—if there are those who suffer guilt for seeking a livelihood in Daemon's territory, let them find comfort in numbers. Let them take consolation from the knowledge that many of our major artists are doing commercials these days—including Orson Welles, Henry Fonda, Robert Morley, Marcel Marceau, and even Sir Laurence Oliver. And if all these great stars do it, it really can't be wrong, can it?

But what about the lack of opportunity to express myself creatively? Isn't it frustrating? Yes, it is. But it's also frustrating not to be able to pay the rent. (A classic conflict that I hereby escalate to a mystery.)

Anyhow, there are occasional opportunities for actors to fulfill themselves in commercials. Why just the other day I created one of the most original characters of my career: I played the voice of a streptococcus infection. I was lurking in Mrs. Simpson's wash, until G-Man Concentrated Super Suds in the Blue Box came in and arrested me.

The revival of radio will once again give many performers an opportunity to function, at least partially, as artists, and at the same time, earn a good living.

For the public the rewards will be greater. Listeners will reclaim an art form that was important and dear to them. Small, portable sets have desocialized the medium and made it even more intimate. You can now hear your favorite radio program on your pillow, or under the covers, or in the bathroom—and innumerable other places where there's just the "two of you." May you live happily ever after.

(Sneak in organ music)

And now, as we leave the air, this is Joe Julian saying I've enjoyed spinning off these memories of my "thirty years before the mike." I hope they have given you some pleasure and an inkling of what it was like behind the scenes in radio's golden age. *(Pause)* I also hope they have whetted your appetite for radio's rejuvenation. But it's true that revival will be sparked only when the moguls are convinced it will pay off; when they hear the sound of money ringing in their ears.

(Sound-effect: coins jingling)

There are signs this is beginning to happen. The moguls are becoming increasingly aware of the vast portion of our population with ears at the ready. There are signs that soon we will no longer be deprived of an art form that flourishes in every other major country in the world.

(*Music up briefly—fade and hold under*)

Trying to analyze the reasons for the broad, universal appeal of radio drama I found it expressed best by a little seven-year-old boy who, during a recent survey on preferences of children, was asked which he liked better, plays on the radio or plays on television.

"On the radio," he said.

"Why?" he was asked.

He thought for a moment, then replied, "Because I can see the pictures better."